Advanced Praise for *Culturally Proficient Leadership: The Personal Journey Begins Within*

By **Raymond D. Terrell and Randall B. Lindsey**

"An excellent text for school leadership classes as well as for those preparing for teacher education. The ability to make change, starting from within, empowers the individual to educate without barriers."

—**Susan M. Lara**
Professor and Vice President for Student Services
The University of Texas of the Permian Basin

"Terrell and Lindsey take a new and refreshing approach. They challenge readers to actively interrogate the effects of their own experience on the way they interact with the diversity of the school."

—**Nicki King**
Youth and Family Development Specialist
University of California, Davis

"Recognizing that our core values are central to our leadership style, this book takes you on a self-reflection journey of cultural competence. The authors' masterful developmental process leads you to a place of social responsibility, which is so critical for the mosaic that defines education today. Everyone connected to schools, from parents to superintendents, needs to take this journey."

—**Rosemary Papa**
Del and Jewell Lewis Chair of Learner Centered Leadership
Northern Arizona University

"Provides an opportunity for individual reflection as opposed to a more social network of exploration. The idea of a cultural autobiography is compelling and necessary for people to truly extend their journey of understanding themselves and others."

—**Denise Seguine**
Chief Academic Officer
Wichita Public Schools, KS

"Every school leader who desires to be a change agent should travel the journey described in this pioneering book. This is a powerful book that will change your life and profession."

—**Ann N. Chlebicki**
Professor
California State University, Dominguez Hills

"This book is like a self-help book that guides you through your own awareness of 'self,' but in this case it is specific to cultural perceptions and education."

—**Monica Uphoff**
Director of Assessment
Coppell Independent School District, TX

"The authors have been brave enough to broach subjects that are usually difficult to confront, and they gently encourage everyone to join them on their journey of love and equity for all learners. Kudos are due!"

—**Lori L. Grossman**
Instructional Coordinator
Houston Independent School District, TX

I dedicate this book to my wife Eloise who has encouraged all of my writing efforts, and to Darren, my grandnephew, who I hope will live in a world that is culturally competent.

—

I dedicate this book to our grandchildren Dakota, Holly, Charley, Kiera, and Jordyn— they and children like them are why we do this work.

—R.

CULTURALLY PROFICIENT LEADERSHIP

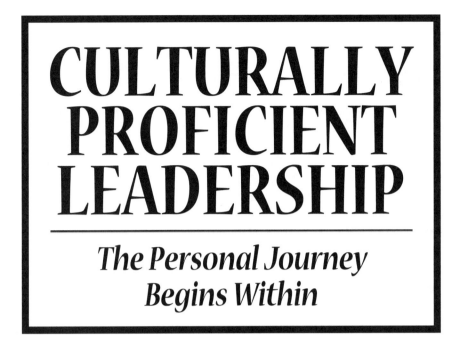

CULTURALLY PROFICIENT LEADERSHIP

The Personal Journey Begins Within

Raymond D. Terrell
Randall B. Lindsey

CORWIN PRESS

A SAGE Company

For information:

Corwin Press
A SAGE Company
2455 Teller Road
Thousand Oaks, California 91320
www.corwinpress.com

SAGE India Pvt. Ltd.
B 1/I 1 Mohan Cooperative
　Industrial Area
Mathura Road, New Delhi 110 044
India

SAGE Ltd.
1 Oliver's Yard
55 City Road
London EC1Y 1SP
United Kingdom

SAGE Asia-Pacific Pte. Ltd.
33 Pekin Street #02-01
Far East Square
Singapore 048763

Printed in the United States of America.

A catalog record of this book is available from the Library of Congress.

978-1-4129-6916-1
978-1-4129-6917-8

This book is printed on acid-free paper.

14　10　9　8　7　6

Acquisitions Editor:	Dan Alpert
Editorial Assistant:	Tatiana Richards
Production Editor:	Eric Garner
Copy Editor:	Gretchen Treadwell
Typesetter:	C&M Digitals (P) Ltd.
Proofreader:	Susan Schon
Indexer:	Jean Casalegno
Cover Designer:	Michael Dubowe

Contents

PART II. KNOWING OURSELVES

Foreword

Michael E. Dantley, EdD

Scholars who have particularly engaged in research in critical race theory, critical feminist theory, and critical Latino(a) theory have explored and articulated the power of personal narratives or storytelling. Personal narratives are not restricted to the vernacular of the scholarly, though they certainly are not immune to academic expression. But personal narratives are products of not only the mind but the heart and the soul of individuals. The stories that are written, spoken, or even sung are the inventions of experience, personal perspectives, and individual predispositions. Daniel Farber and Suzanna Sherry, in their chapter entitled Telling Stories Out of School: An Essay on Narratives in Richard Delgado's edited volume, *Critical Race Theory: The Cutting Edge,* assert that for many, the art of storytelling is not often found in more formal types of literature, but storytelling can tell a counter-hegemonic narrative that questions and holds suspect the tenets of the metanarratives that have so often been celebrated as societal truths. The art of storytelling has a distinct way of blending fact and nuance, perception and reality, and in many ways serves a revisionist or even more significantly at times an unvarnished role in recounting events or life impacting episodes. Telling personal narratives is a vivid example of what Charles Lawrence, III, in quoting Vincent Harding, calls the paradigm of the Word. Lawrence offers several purposes of the Word. According to Lawrence, the Word is a unifying force. The Word is often a "statement of protest, it is an expression of courage, an organizing tool, the articulation of utopian dreams or a higher law . . ." (p. 337). The form and substance of the Word, especially through the art of storytelling, must articulate what we see, what we feel, and what we think. The Word is responsible for describing how we experience life and for disclosing the union of imagination and contextual detail.

In this book, *Culturally Proficient Leadership: The Journey Begins Within,* the authors, Raymond Terrell and Randall Lindsey, have taken the courageous steps to disclose their personal journeys that have led them to become two of the most prolific writers on cultural proficiency and educational leadership in the nation. It is intriguing to discover some of the intersections and similarities of experiences that mark these scholars' journeys. They have clearly had separate points of departure and innumerable differences in experiences. As one is an African American man and the other a white man, it is exceptionally plausible that in multiple ways their journeys would be divergent. But I invite you as you read this poignant text to notice carefully the points of convergence. Pay close attention to the ways in which Terrell's and Lindsey's paths crossed and how the differences in their experiences have helped them to coalesce and explore an area of leadership that can be explosive, aggravating, and powerfully life changing all at the same time.

To couch leadership in a culturally proficient space and to then reveal how these two authors have come to this place of holding school leaders accountable for examining their own dispositions that often minimize and silence others on the basis of difference is a daring project that catapults educational leadership to a totally different arena. It is impossible to think about leadership in a traditional fashion once you have been exposed to the notions of cultural proficiency and the personal narratives of Terrell and Lindsey. It is vitally important for the reader to be open to the narratives and personal perspectives that fill this text while at the same time meeting the challenge of juxtaposing your own stories that tell of your journey in leadership as well. The exciting facet of the art of storytelling and in particular the work of Terrell and Lindsey in this text is that the reader is encouraged to listen to the authors' personal narratives while also being encouraged to create his or her own. The authors leave open the door to legitimate our own personal experiences and to use them all as fodder for creating the context and content of our leadership journeys.

Reading this text allows us to celebrate our imaginations, clarify our perspectives and locate ourselves through testimonies and narratives where the awesome work of culturally proficient leadership is concerned. Terrell and Lindsey motivate us to position leadership in an intimate space colored by our experiences and perceptions. We are challenged to interrogate those experiences and perceptions through the lens of cultural proficiency, openness to difference and celebration of the Other. This text is an intellectual as well as introspective journey designed to cause leaders to couch their personal and professional behaviors in a context of understanding, appreciation, and recognition of difference and diversity. The authors compel us to grapple with the fact that leadership really is a journey that begins within.

Preface

. . . I believe deeply that we cannot solve the challenges of our time unless we solve them together—unless we perfect our union by understanding that we may have different stories, but we hold common hopes; that we may not look the same and may not come from the same place, but we all want to move in the same direction: toward a better future for our children and our grandchildren.

—Senator Barack Obama,
(*Los Angeles Times*, 2008)

The epigraph above, in combination with the epigraph to Chapter 5 referencing President Bush's acknowledgment of historical discrimination in our country, provides the rationale for this book. We excerpted passages from our autobiographies that illustrate some of our earliest recollections of our own racial identity as well as those who are different from us. Please read the passage below as an introduction to us via excerpts from our "stories."

Excerpts From Ray and Randy's Autobiographies

Ray's Excerpt

My mother worked as a domestic for one of the community's leading white families and my father was a laborer at a steel mill in a neighboring community. My parents' relationship was stable. Because both parents worked, it was my perception that we were fairly well off, a black family not experiencing any of the usual indicators of poverty . . . disconnected utilities, a lack of food, and we had one of the first televisions in our neighborhood. My mom had a fifth grade education and I discovered that she had difficulty reading when I brought her a note from high school and she had me read it to her. My dad had a sixth grade education but he was an avid reader and followed current events in the newspaper and by listening to daily newscasts.

The fact that they worked two very different jobs afforded them very different social perspectives and worldviews, and both of them freely shared their perspectives with me. As a domestic for a powerful family in the community, my mom viewed the world as a very dangerous place for African American males. She constantly admonished me to be sure to be polite and show deference to white people in order to avoid confrontations that could ultimately prove to be deadly. There was no one at my father's workplace that had any community connections. He felt that he had a social responsibility to challenge the status quo around issues of social justice and constantly challenged the segregated school setting and other forms of local discrimination. It was confusing, to say the least, to constantly get input from such divergent points of view, while at the same time experience exclusion from local eateries, athletic facilities, and other public venues.

My father taught me how to identify and question level one issues. He was considered to be a radical for those times around local issues. I failed to grasp the breadth or depth of the scope of racism. Living in a very narrowly defined space and place and being internally focused, masked how racism negatively impacted the lives of everybody. I clearly had no notion that whites, though impacted differently, were also negatively affected by acquiring an inflated sense of privilege and entitlement.

Randy's Excerpt

My first recollection of race was as a small child. I lived with my parents in a shotgun-style house that was located on the "other side" of the railroad tracks, behind a factory, in a neighborhood that was racially mixed. We were white, and there were three groups we now call demographic groups—our labels were "colored people," the Irish, and we who were from "mid-southern" states. The period was the late 1940s and early 1950s. The black men and the southern white men worked in one of the three factories in town . . .

We all lived in this largely unimproved neighborhood . . . I never regarded it as a hard life because it wasn't. That was our life. Our house was clean and neat and I assumed that was the case for all the other families in our neighborhood.

The odd thing was that we did very little visiting with those who were not like us. My father was always clear at the mistreatment of Negroes in the larger society. Neither of my parents went beyond eighth grade in their formal education. When he retired, my father had worked forty years in a foundry. My mom worked primarily in the home, except for a few years that she worked in a department store when my sister and I were in high school . . . My thinking about matters of race developed when I was quite young.

Our complete cultural autobiographies are in the Appendices. You may be tempted to read them before reading the body of this book. Please read this book in the manner and sequence that works best for you. We wish for you to use this book as your guide to viewing leadership as a continuous growth process.

Acknowledgments

Ray and Randy are deeply appreciative of the many people who have influenced and shaped our lives. We are deeply grateful for the support and patience of family, friends, and colleagues who encouraged us at every stage in the development of this book. In constructing this book we were keenly aware that we are the sum total of our experiences, and it has been educators as mentors and as colleagues who started us on our continuous journey to cultural proficiency. What began as an effort to "tell our story" has evolved into a deepening appreciation for our friendship.

A special thank you goes to Dan Alpert, our acquisitions editor, for being with us in this journey. It was Dan's abiding interest in the concept for this book that provided us the encouragement to stay with our dream. Appreciation also goes to Rachel Livsey, our acquisitions editor at the time of the book proposal, for her encouragement to write this book.

This book would not have the conceptual framework of cultural proficiency without the work of Terry Cross, Kikanza Nuri Robins, Delores Lindsey, Laraine Roberts, Franklin CampbellJones, Richard Martinez, Stephanie Graham, R. Chris Westphal, Jr., and Cynthia Jew. This book was informed and shaped by their foregoing work on cultural competence and cultural proficiency.

Delores B. Lindsey is deeply appreciated for her contributions to this book. Delores provided many hours of feedback on each stage of the final manuscript. Her knowledge of the subject, skills with editorial feedback, passion for this work, and insights to each of us contributed mightily to this manuscript. We thank Kikanza Nuri Robins who continues to provide friendship and feedback to all stages of our work. We also thank Henri Mondschein from California Lutheran University who read our initial autobiographies and strongly encouraged our work.

Corwin Press gratefully acknowledges the contributions of the following reviewers:

Lori L. Grossman
Instructional Coordinator
ECH and Mentoring Professional Development Services
Houston Independent School District
Houston, TX

Kathryn McCormick
Seventh Grade Teacher
Gahanna Middle School East
Westerville, OH

Christi Roach
Executive Director
Oklahoma Association of Elementary School Principals
Oklahoma City, OK

Denise Seguine
Chief Academic Officer
Wichita Public Schools
Wichita, KS

Monica Uphoff
Director of Assessment
Coppell Independent School District
Coppell, TX

About the Authors

Raymond D. Terrell, EdD, is the Assistant Dean, Research and Diversity, and a member of the Department of Educational Leadership at Miami University in Oxford, Ohio. He has served as a high school and junior high school English teacher, an elementary school principal, and an assistant superintendent in public schools in Ohio. He spent one year as a faculty member at Texas A&M University in the Department of Educational Administration. He spent nineteen years at California State University—fourteen in the Department of Educational Administration and for five years he was the Dean of the School of Education. Ray has thirty-five years of professional experience with diversity and equity issues. He has served school districts in California, Arizona, Nevada, Michigan, Ohio, Pennsylvania, and Indiana. Ray writes about issues of diversity, inclusion, and equity.

Ray lives in Woodlawn, Ohio, with his wife Eloise. They have two adult children, Dina and William (terrelr@muohio.edu).

Randall B. Lindsey, PhD, is Emeritus Professor, California State University, Los Angeles, and has a practice centered on educational consulting and issues related to diversity. Currently, he is coordinator of an EdD cohort in Los Angeles for the School of Education, California Lutheran University, where he served as Interim Dean. He has served as a teacher, an administrator, executive director of a nonprofit corporation, as Distinguished Educator in Residence at Pepperdine University, and as Chair of the Education Department at the University of Redlands. All of Randy's experiences have been in working with diverse populations and his area of study is the behavior of white people in multicultural settings. It is his belief and experience that too often white people are observers of multicultural issues rather than personally involved with them. To that end, he designs and implements interventions that address the roles of all sectors of the society.

Randy and his wife and frequent coauthor, Delores, are enjoying this phase of life as grandparents, as educators, and in support of just causes (randallblindsey@aol.com).

Introduction

Dear Reader,

As the authors of this book we thank you for your interest in the topic of culturally proficient leadership. It is our intent with this book to provide an approach to leadership and self-discovery that you may experience as fresh, creative, and relevant. In writing this book we have endeavored to provide you the opportunity to:

- explore and learn "how" and "from whom" you developed your assumptions, values, and beliefs about people culturally different from you
- learn from people who are culturally different from you
- develop an intentional frame for culturally proficient leadership practice

HOW THIS BOOK CAME TO BE

The two of us have been educators since the mid-1960s. We began as junior high school teachers, Ray in Cincinnati, Ohio, and Randy in Kankakee, Illinois. Over the next few years, we progressed to becoming administrators of school desegregation projects and university faculty members. We have had the wonderful opportunity of working together as colleagues to pursue our own growth as equity advocates and to work with many schools and other agencies as they strove to meet the needs of our increasingly diverse and demographically changing student populations.

We are now at that point in our careers and personal lives where we are reflecting on the many experiences we have had—some successful, some less than successful—that have all contributed to our continuous growth as citizens of this country and as educators within public school systems.

Ours is the story of a black man and a white man who came together in 1970 and fostered a personal and professional friendship that continues to grow to this day. From Kankakee to Cincinnati to Los Angeles, we have been together as we continue to expand our consciousness about issues of diversity, access, inclusion, and systems of oppression. Over the years we have had the opportunity to work with many PreK–12 and university educators who have been our allies in doing this work. Principal among those colleagues are our coauthors in writing the cultural proficiency books—Kikanza Nuri Robins, Delores B. Lindsey, Franklin CampbellJones, Laraine Roberts, Richard S. Martinez, Stephanie Graham, R. Chris Westphal, Jr., Cynthia L. Jew, Linda Jungwirth, and Jarvis VNC Pahl. We are indebted to what we have learned from and with each of our friends.

In October 2005, we met in Ray's home in Cincinnati and began to write our stories. We were not sure what would come of it, other than a therapeutic rendering of our travels before and since we met and chose to be partners in working within school systems to lessen the negative effects of oppression. For three days, we sat in separate rooms at our laptop computers and constructed our cultural autobiographies. We met frequently during the day to talk about writing our journeys but not to read one another's "stories." On the fourth day, we decided we had many experiences, rendered as our "stories," that may be of interest, if not outright value, to readers like you who are taking their "equity journeys."

IS THIS BOOK FOR YOU?

This book is for you if you are an educational leader and serve as a teacher, counselor, administrator, professor, university supervisor, teacher aide, custodian, playground supervisor, parent, guardian, school board member, or other interested member of the community. This book is about you as a formal or nonformal leader in the community you serve. In the context of this particular book, your role is not important. What is important is the difference you want to make and are making in the lives of our children, youth, and adult learners.

Given that many of you reading this book may not have even been born when we started teaching, we assumed that much of our early experiences are matters of history to you. Others reading may have been personally affected by school desegregation and were some of the children and youth on those school buses in the 1970s or later. It is because of the historical nature of our personal journeys that we believe we may be able to guide you in your journey to becoming a culturally proficient leader.

This book is organized to:

- provide a glimpse of the recent history of equity movements and how they have impacted public schools and leadership within those schools
- use our journeys/stories as vignettes to illustrate and amplify your growing awareness of and facility with equity issues
- provide you a set of protocols and instruments to record your equity story—both the one you know and the one you have yet to live
- provide you with the means to make intentional choices about the focus of your leadership efforts

Some have lived it; others study it! Our hope is for you to create your own leadership equity story.

THIS BOOK IS A PERSONAL JOURNEY OF WILL AND SKILL

This book is an appeal to the moral centeredness of embracing leadership as a very personal journey of commitment and vision. Cross's (Cross, Bazron, Dennis, & Isaacs, 1989) "inside-out" feature of cultural proficiency becomes a first step in one's personal transformation that can lead to systemic educational reform. This inside-out feature of cultural proficiency combines Hilliard's (1991) notion of "will" with Schon's (1983) "skill" of reflective practice.

Many approaches to leadership development rely on reflective practice (Schein, 1989; Schon, 1983; Senge et al., 2000; Wheatley, 1994). Reflective practice is a powerful tool to identify one's values and behaviors prior to making needed changes in educational policies and practices (Senge, 2000). However, it was Hilliard's (1991) challenge of asking if we had the will to educate all children, and his evocation of "will" as a moral construct that began to get notice in mainstream educational leadership circles. More than a decade later, Fullan (2003) went so far as to label the education of all children to be a "moral imperative."

In preparing this manuscript, we took stock of our own careers in doing equity-related work and wrote our cultural autobiographies. In writing our autobiographies, which we freely refer to as our "stories," we learned that our careers have been ones of discovery and of teaching. Freire's (1987) observation that *there is no teaching without learning* is wholly applicable to our lives, both personal and professional. As we examined our autobiographies, the framework for this book emerged in a manner that we believe will inform people like you who are interested in being increasingly effective in cross-cultural settings. This book provides frequent opportunities for you to reflect on how your attitudes and values about culture and leadership have been developed, and to construct new knowledge for continuing to become more effective leaders in cross-cultural settings.

We discovered that the progression from segregation to cultural competence and proficiency is the path *our* lives are taking. Our respective awareness of race, then gender, and, in turn, other cultural experiences may not be the same sequence in your life. Rather, our notion with this book is for you to reflect on your cultural learnings and how your learning informs the leader you are today and provides you with information to be intentional in choosing to be the leader you will be tomorrow.

WHY IS THIS BOOK NECESSARY?

The assessment and accountability measures that have emerged in recent years have led to a new, fresh look at standards-based leadership and accountability in the context of diverse schools. Since the *Brown v. Topeka Board of Education* decision by the U.S. Supreme Court in 1954, educational leaders have tiptoed around how best to serve the needs of our nation of diverse learners. Fullan (2003) identified the moral imperative of formal school leaders being responsible for all schools in their districts. Many authors have identified leadership characteristics, knowledge, and skills needed in our schools (Marzano, Pickering, & Pollock, 2001; Reeves, 2006; Singleton & Linton, 2006). Irrespective of the change model, school reform initiative, or current mandates, school leaders must first be willing to explore their core values, beliefs, and assumptions about serving all students' needs.

Cultural proficiency is based in the notion that personal and organizational leadership is an Inside-Out process (Cross et al., 1989). In our earlier works (Lindsey, Graham, Westphal, & Jew, 2008; Lindsey, Martinez, & Lindsey, 2007; Lindsey, Nuri Robins, & Terrell, 2003; Lindsey, Roberts, & CampbellJones, 2005), we described and provided models for leadership that have been well received by PreK–12 educators and faculty from university leadership preparation programs. This manuscript adds to those works by providing the reader with a clear road map for leadership as a personal journey.

Culturally proficient leadership is distinguished from other leadership approaches in that it is anchored in the belief that a leader must clearly understand one's own assumptions, beliefs, and values about people and cultures different from one's self in order to be effective in cross-cultural settings.

In this book, we use our personal journeys of cultural identity exploration and discovery as a guide for you, the reader, to consider yourself within the context of the communities you serve and lead. This book begins and ends with a focus on one's self with the premise that one cannot adequately lead change in schools or other organizations until one truly knows and understands one's self as a leader.

HOW TO USE THIS BOOK

We organized this book in three parts to guide you in your journey toward cultural proficiency:

- The balance of Part I is comprised of three chapters that describe the importance of school leadership, the four tools of cultural proficiency, and opportunity for you to construct your cultural autobiography.
- Part II consists of three chapters in which you are guided through processes of reflection and interviews to deepen your knowledge of

cross-cultural relationships of race, ethnicity, national origin, language, gender, socioeconomic status, sexual orientation, and ableness.

- Part III contains two chapters. Chapter 7 guides you to synthesize material from the previous chapters and Chapter 8 is our encouragement to you as a leader in our schools and communities.

We wish you well as you continue on your journey to learn about yourself as a member of our diverse United States.

Part I

Leadership as an Informed Personal Perspective

The Leadership Journey Begins Within

1

The more things change, the more they stay the same.

—Anonymous

GETTING CENTERED

In selecting this book, you have indicated your interest in education, leadership, and/or issues of equity and diversity. Most likely you are regarded as a formal or a nonformal leader in your school or community. So, what is it that caused you to open this book and read this far? We invite you to record your initial thoughts to these questions. Your responses will serve as important guides through this journey with us.

_____

_____

_____

_____

Though educators and students may be in the same classroom and school at the same time, very often we are strangers to one another. Where underachievement is prevalent in a school, the cultural differences between educator and students are often represented by contrasting experiences, values, beliefs, language, socioeconomics, and worldviews. Educators and students treat one another differently because of the lack of shared experiences.

The reality of different experiences is exacerbated by the fact that many people in our society still live segregated lives based on race/ethnicity, class, and linguistic patterns. To be effective cross-culturally, we must fully understand that cultural realities are sets of lived, learned experiences. Lisa Delpit (1996) eloquently expressed it with these words, *All the students that we teach are "Other People's Children."* Since we cannot live each other's cultures, it becomes imperative that we begin our leadership journey by looking inward to ourselves and understanding our reactions to people who are culturally different from us. To understand ourselves as cultural beings is a necessary step to effectively teach "Other Peoples' Children."

This chapter is designed for you to reflect on your leadership role in your school. In the next few pages, we invite you to begin this journey toward cultural proficiency by:

- taking a look at your school and your reactions to what you see
- considering the equity issues that abide in your school
- considering access and achievement gaps as leadership issues
- viewing aspects of current legislation such as No Child Left Behind (NCLB) as useful tools

TAKING A LOOK AT MY SCHOOL AND WHAT I SEE (AND DON'T SEE)

As school leaders, we inherit schools and school districts that are influenced by social, political, and economic forces not readily apparent. Most likely you began your education career as a classroom teacher and entered your first school with unbridled enthusiasm to do your very best work. In your preparation program, you took the required history and philosophy courses, and may or may not have fully related what was taught in those courses to be forces that impinge on your school and your classroom. Your first school assignment may have ranked anywhere along a continuum of being "extremely pleased" to "extremely displeased." Things spoken and unspoken made you react to students and colleagues in your school.

Envision yourself driving to and from your current school. Take note of the neighborhood and the services present, or not present, for your students. Also, note whether or not you would live in the neighborhoods of your students. Do the visible elements of the neighborhood environment cause you to judge your students and their parents? Underlying the visible elements of our school communities are unapparent forces that make even more impact on our students, our schools, and ourselves. These seemingly invisible historical forces contribute to the sense of privilege or deprivation experienced in our schools that creates stress for your students, their parents or guardians, and for you. These invisible forces are the "equity issues" that serve as the great unspoken in our profession as well as in society at large. The commonly used metaphor to describe these invisible forces is "equity issues are the elephant in the middle of the room that we pretend not to see."

Reflection

Describe your school environment. Describe the community outside the school's boundary. What do you think and feel about the effect of these environments? Please use the space below to record your thoughts and feelings.

_____

_____

_____

_____

ARE THERE "EQUITY ISSUES" IN YOUR SCHOOL?

How much do you know about equity issues in your school or in schools throughout our country? To what extent are historical events of inequity present in your school today? Are students in your school well served by the academic and cocurricular programs? As you read this section, keep these questions before you and use the space at the end to record your responses. Remember, one of the major purposes of this book is to become increasingly aware of your reactions to people whose life experiences may be different from yours.

Reaction to equity issues is often dependent on one's own experiences as a student. Those of us who have benefited from the current school structure may have a reaction that is different from those of us who were marginalized or made invisible. The twin topics of universal public education and equity in education have yielded very different experiences for cultural groups of students both historically and currently.

Miscommunication and stress among educators can often be traced to how well or poorly people felt served in their own school experiences. Similarly, educators who have been well served in our school systems often are at odds with parents and other community members who have been less well served. Irrespective of your prior personal experiences, to be a school leader today, knowledge of the historical context of access and equity issues will provide an important context on which to build your vision for what our schools can and must be.

Two expressed values in our democracy not yet fully realized are universal pubic education through high school and equitable educational opportunities. Mistakenly thought by many educators to be a requirement in all fifty states, required education through high school or age eighteen is a post-World War II phenomenon that continues to unfold across the country (Hudson, 1999; Kousser, 1984). The National Center for Educational Statistics (2005) reported that as of 2002, twenty-seven states have compulsory education requirements to the attainment of age sixteen.

Progress toward universal education is intertwined with the advancement in equitable treatment and equal outcomes for students based on gender, race, ethnicity, language, and ableness also has been evolving. Legal issues such as *Brown v. Topeka Board of Education* (1954) and *Serrano v. Priest* (1971, 1976, 1977) (as cited in Townley & Schmeider-Ramirez, 2007) set in motion processes designed to remedy inequities intentionally structured into our society and, consequently, our school systems. Executive measures such as the order issued by President Eisenhower in 1967 that sent U.S. paratroopers to insure the integration of Central High School, Little Rock, Arkansas, and legislative measures such as the 1964 Civil Rights Act were intended to confront historical inequities. While dismantling the legal barriers to segregation has been a monumental achievement, having schools be successful for all students is a dream still deferred for many.

Prominent researchers and social commentators have pressed the issue for equity in our schools for two generations. Edmonds (1979) identified correlates for schools effective for all students, yet we continue to "discover" those factors as new. Hilliard (1991) challenged us and asked if we had "the will" to educate all children. Kozol (1991; 2005; 2007) continues to describe what is happening in too many schools with the terms "shame" and "savage inequalities." Berliner (2005) makes a compelling and chilling case for the intransigence of poverty and its effect on our schools, educational policy, and society. Importantly, Berliner (2005) illustrates the intersection of poverty *and* race/ethnicity that undercuts the notion prevalent in some professional development circles that the achievement gap is only a socioeconomic issue.

Reflection

Take a few moments and consider the questions posed at the beginning of this section and repeated here: How much do you know about equity issues in your school or in schools throughout our country? To what extent are historical events of inequity present in your school today? Are students in your school well served by the academic and cocurricular programs? Please record your responses in the space below.

_____

_____

_____

_____

CONFRONTING THE "GAPS" AS A LEADERSHIP ISSUE

At the dawn of the twenty-first century, we are now faced with the challenge to lead schools in ways that provide equitable opportunities irrespective of students' cultural memberships. Schools are naturally heterogeneous to address issues of equity. We bring together students from different cultural groups of race, socioeconomic status, gender, and sexual orientation with the intent to provide quality education. Bridging achievement gaps is a complex undertaking that requires leaders who have knowledge of the social dynamics within society and our schools that foster disparities.

Lay people and educators similarly mention the achievement gap as though it is the single phenomenon of test scores. For that reason, we use the term "educational gaps" throughout this book. Educational achievement is comprised of two components within schools' control—(1) schools providing access to high quality curriculum and instruction to all students, and (2) outcome measures that assess student achievement. To illustrate the frailty of relying on outcome measures alone, one has only to examine the work of early researchers such as Coleman (1966) and Jencks (Jencks, Smith, Acland, & Bane, 1972) who pointed to the difference in African Americans and white students' performance and implicated genetic inferiority, poverty, and lack of family support as the reasons for underachievement. In effect, they held that something was wrong with the students, their families, or their cultures. Not addressing systemic access disparities of high quality educational programs, experienced teachers, and equitable school funding resulted in a continuance of the status quo of some students being well served and others less well, if at all.

The reality is that school systems across the country have seldom treated students in an equitable manner. Systemic inequities predate the landmark *Brown v. Topeka Board of Education* (1954) that was to end "separate but equal"; however, disparities continue to persist in the form of current funding inequities in many states even today. Funding alone, however, will not create a level playing field. A fundamental change in the way that many students are educated must occur or we will lose another generation of youth to poverty and/or lives of crime.

Our PreK–12 (pre-kindergarten through twelfth grade) student population in the U.S. is growing steadily with the greatest growth being demographic groups who have been underserved historically. Predictably, students of color and English Learners will soon comprise 40 percent of all students in our nation's PreK–12 schools. In many schools and districts these populations are 90–100 percent of the student population, as patterns of segregation seem to grow. In contrast, the educator population remains overwhelmingly white, middle class, and female. Therefore, the reality is that the primary culture of U.S. schools continues to reflect a Eurocentric, middle class, and standard English speaking paradigm (Milner IV, 2007). Students who enter our schools and share the values, beliefs, socioeconomic status, behaviors, worldview, language, and degree of ableness that most closely align with this dominant paradigm tend to be most successful. The question we must ask ourselves as school leaders and answer in meaningful ways is, *How do we meet the academic and social needs of young people who enter our schools with a different set of values, beliefs, socioeconomic experiences, behaviors, worldview, home languages, and degrees of ableness?*

As you think about your school, what inequities do you think might exist? How do you describe the behavior of formal and nonformal leaders in addressing inequities? How do you describe your behavior? Please use the space below to record your responses.

_____

_____

_____

_____

NCLB AS A LEADERSHIP TOOL

Selected aspects of No Child Left Behind (NCLB; 2002) can serve as a tool to support access and equity efforts. NCLB as the current version of the Elementary and Secondary Education Act has made the general public more aware of differential educational opportunity and achievement patterns that exist in and among our schools and communities. Within our schools, we now have the opportunity to discuss and analyze student achievement and access issues as part of our everyday educational practice. Resistance and selective blindness that existed a few years ago is being replaced in some schools as faculty come together to examine student achievement and access issues that previously had been the "elephant in the middle of the room." Though resistance continues, thoughtful and committed educational leaders are skillfully using NCLB as a pretext for addressing achievement gap issues.

The oft-touted achievement gap is, in reality, a multifaceted outcome measure of gaps in access to education. The light that NCLB has shined on differential achievement patterns now points to multiple achievement gaps. Achievement gaps differentiated by race/ethnicity, gender, class, language, and degree of physical and mental ableness are now highlighted in the popular media. The focus on different aspects of achievement gaps has rekindled interest in examining who gets suspended, expelled, and otherwise excluded from "regular" classrooms. The examination of who attends school regularly as well as who drops out or is "pushed out" is being undertaken by schools nationwide. Data such as disparities in achievement patterns, dropout rates, and enrollment in higher order courses are powerful when used as indicators of access barriers that exist within the school. However, it takes the courageous leader to be able to change the focus from "what is wrong with the student" to "what is it we need to do differently to meet students needs."

We propose a process of developing an intentional leadership perspective guided by personally and internally asking you the following questions:

1. Who am I, a school leader, as a cultural being?

2. What are my values, beliefs, behaviors, language, class, race/ethnicity, and worldview?

3. What values, beliefs, behavior, language, class, race/ethnicity, and worldview do the various students bring to my classroom/school?

4. How does my culture affect the students who come to my classroom/school?

5. How will the students' cultures affect me?

6. What must I do when my culture and the students' culture is different?

Your responses to these questions become the basis for the cultural autobiography you will write in Chapter 3. The reflections and personal interviews you will complete in Chapters 4–6 will deepen your understanding of those culturally different from you and why you regard them as you do. You will experience your reflections, your interviews, and your final assembling of this information as a deeply personal and liberating educational journey. You will come to know yourself even better, to understand the basis for your values and beliefs, and to be intentional about being the leader you want to be.

DEFINITIONS OF KEY TERMS

Understanding key terms is important to effective communication. Do you recall your first year teaching and the first parent night or parent-teacher conference and how you rattled off terms and acronyms that the parents/guardians didn't seem to know? You may have used terms such as "standards-based assessment" or "polynomial fractions" or "continuous progress." Acronyms that may have tripped off your tongue could have been ELD, EL, IEP, or NCTE. Yes, of course, each profession has its own terminology and acronyms.

Cultural proficiency has terms to be defined, too. From the very beginning of our work together, Ray held that "the ultimate power in society is the power to define." For that reason, you might ask, why do we take space and time to define seemingly common terms? The answer is because some educators and laypeople choose to be culturally blind about equity and diversity-related perspectives and derisively dismiss them as "politically correct." We experience two uses of political correctness: (1) people in our profession who have no interest in learning how to be successful with some cultural groups of students and use political correctness as a reason not to change and (2) people who mask their ineffectiveness through use of *au courant* words and phrases but display little or no commitment to the deeper values of access and equity. We find that, though the motivation of the speakers may be dissimilar, their impact on students' education is similarly ineffective. Therefore, we offer the following key terms and definitions for our use in schools.

Culture: We define culture as involving far more than ethnic or racial differences. Culture is the set of practices and beliefs shared by members of a particular group that distinguish that group from other groups. Culture includes all characteristics of human description including age, gender, socioeconomic status, geography, ancestry, religion, language, history, sexual orientation, physical and mental level of ableness, occupation, and other affiliations.

Cultural Informancy: This reflects our experience of having cross-cultural relationships that are authentic and trusting and allow for mutual learning and feedback that leads to personal growth.

Demographic Groups: Due to the historical stigma that continues to impact our communities and schools, we use the term "demographic group" in place of the term "subgroup." Every few years the eugenics debate and terms such as subspecies and related uses of the prefix "sub" are used in racist, discriminatory ways. We find the term "demographic group" to be more precise and accurate.

Dominant Culture: It should be noted that the dominant culture paradigm that permeates schools tends to be present in most schools regardless of the communities where they are located. Every classroom has a great deal of cultural diversity present. By our definition, some cultures are readily visible while others may be hidden and not apparent. When we examine achievement, suspension, and expulsion data; assignment to certain categories of special education; or the lack of assignment to gifted, accelerated and advanced placement classes, it becomes clear that those who bring a different culture to the school do not receive equitable treatment and fail to attain equal levels of success.

Equity: Access to material and human resources in proportion to needs. Once disparities have been identified, if we proceed with equal allocation of resources, the disparities continue. Equitable allocation responds to identified needs. An example well documented in too many of our schools is veteran teachers working with the most successful students and new, inexperienced, and, too often, ineffective teachers being assigned to work with struggling students. Very often the same is true of principal assignments.

Ethnicity: From Lindsey, Nuri Robins, & Terrell (2003) we quote, " . . . ancestral heritage and geography, common history, and, to some degree, physical appearance" (p. 41).

National Origin: A designation used in the 1964 Civil Rights Act to specify that people were not to be discriminated against due to their country of birth or prior citizenship.

Nativism: The practice of valuing the rights of citizens born in this country over those of immigrants. This practice was promulgated throughout the U.S. during the nineteenth century to marginalize the waves of immigrants from Ireland, Germany, and Eastern Europe.

Race: Also from Lindsey et al. (2003) we quote, "*Race* is a concept developed by social scientists and misinterpreted by eugenicists and social Darwinists in the [19th] century to characterize people by their physical features and to use those differences to justify the subjugation of people of color and perpetuate the domination of the white race" (p. 41).

Reflection: Careful consideration of one's behaviors, plans, values, or assumptions in an effort to improve interpersonal and professional practice.

Sexual Orientation: An enduring emotional, romantic, sexual, or affectional attraction to another person. It is easily distinguished from other components of sexuality including biological sex, gender identity (the psychological sense of being male or female), and the social gender role (adherence to cultural norms for feminine and masculine behavior).

Sexual orientation exists along a continuum that ranges from exclusive homosexuality to exclusive heterosexuality and includes various forms of bisexuality. Bisexual persons can experience sexual, emotional, and affectional attraction to both their own sex and the opposite sex. Persons with a homosexual orientation are sometimes referred to as gay (both men and women) or as lesbian (women only).

Sexual orientation is different from sexual behavior because it refers to feelings and self-concept. Persons may or may not express their sexual orientation in their behaviors.

Reflection

We invite you to turn back to the questions and comments that you recorded on the first page of this chapter and take a few minutes in the space provided and record new thoughts, feelings, comments, or questions that are with you now.

_____

_____

_____

_____

Chapter 2 provides an overview of the tools of cultural proficiency. The tools and the associated reflections provide you with an important lens and key concepts as you continue your leadership journey. Take your time. Enjoy the journey within. You and your communities will benefit from your journey.

The Cultural Proficiency Leadership Lens

2

The two sides of the continuum remind me of Jim Collins's "window-mirror" analogy—leaders who peer out the window see "others" as being problematic, whereas leaders who look into the mirror peer into themselves for answers in how to work with those who are culturally different from themselves.

—Dana Rivers, Los Angeles
Unified School District (October 6, 2007)

GETTING CENTERED

Have you ever read a school's mission statement that purports "all students will achieve to high levels" and wondered to yourself, "then why don't all demographic groups of students achieve to high levels at this school?" Do you ever hear the cacophonous sound of fellow educators talking about students at your school in ways that are unhealthy and you don't say anything? What do you say or wish you had said? What does it sound like when fellow educators are engaged in healthy conversation about their practice? Please write your responses to these questions in the space below:

_____

_____

_____

_____

We view our work, as the authors of this book, as bringing us all together in the understanding that educational gaps are ***our*** issue with at least three agreements being important prerequisites:

- First, we must acknowledge that educational gaps are historical and persistent. These gaps were in our schools when we arrived, we inherited them, *but we may not ignore them.* The issue of the academic underperformance of children of poverty, African American, Latino, and First Nations[1] students is not new information.
- Second, if the gaps are to be closed, as well-intentioned and well-informed educators and laypersons, we must step forward as leaders to examine our values and behaviors and the policies and practices of our schools.
- Third, we can make a difference for our students and their communities when we listen to who our students say they are and what their needs are. Too often our needs or the needs of the school system take precedent.

With these agreements, you are fully prepared to explore cultural proficiency as a set of tools to serve you as a responsible person in society, as an effective educator, and as a leader to other educators. In this chapter we present the tools of cultural proficiency for you to understand yourself as a leader, and your school as an organizational culture in service of students from cultures different from yours.

In this chapter we introduce cultural proficiency as:

- a process that begins with us, not with our students or their communities
- a shift in thinking, for some educators, that moves us from viewing culture as problematic to embracing and esteeming culture
- a lens through which we view our role as educators
- a concept comprised of a set of four interrelated tools to guide our practice

CULTURAL PROFICIENCY IS AN INSIDE-OUT PROCESS

Cross et al. (1989) refers to cultural proficiency being an *inside-out process* of personal and organizational change. Cultural proficiency is who we are, more than what we do. Effective use of the tools of cultural proficiency is predicated on your ability and willingness to recognize that change is an inside-out process in which we are students of our assumptions about self, others, and the context in which we work with others.

It is our intent to guide you in this book in such a way that you will reflect on your actions, the actions of your school, and the cultural communities you serve. This book engages your leadership journey with many activities that have the following in common:

- You will recognize your own assumptions and retain those that facilitate culturally proficient actions and change those that impede such actions.
- You will apply this inside-out process to examine and change, as appropriate, school policies and practices that either impede or facilitate culturally proficient ends.

The willingness and ability to examine yourself and your organization is fundamental to addressing educational gap issues. Cultural proficiency provides a comprehensive, systemic structure for school leaders to identify, examine, and discuss educational issues in our schools. The four tools of cultural proficiency, described later in this chapter, provide you with the means to assess and change your values and behaviors, and your school's policies and practices, in ways that serve our students, schools, communities, and society. Your leadership journey using cultural proficiency as a means for self-growth begins with mastery of four tools as a philosophical imperative.

CULTURAL PROFICIENCY REPRESENTS A LEADERSHIP PARADIGM

Cultural proficiency is a mindset for how we interact with all people, irrespective of their cultural memberships. Cultural proficiency is a worldview that carries explicit values, language, and standards for effective personal interactions and professional practices. Cultural proficiency is a 24/7 approach to our personal and professional lives. Most important, cultural proficiency is *not* a set of independent activities or strategies that you learn to use with others—your students, colleagues, or community members.

Too often, we meet and work with educators looking for shortcuts to working with people who are culturally different from them. It is our experience that educators seeking shortcuts to working in cross-cultural settings have an innate belief in their own superiority and view others as needing to be changed. Cross et al. (1989) was motivated to develop cultural competence and cultural proficiency when he recognized that mental health professionals and institutions were ineffective in cross-cultural settings. More recently Milner IV (2007), in presenting a framework for educational researchers, suggests that "researchers and participants engage in reflection together to think through what is happening in a particular research community, with race and culture placed at the core" (p. 396).

Educators who commit to culturally proficient practices represent a paradigmatic shift away from the current, dominant group view of regarding "underperforming" cultural demographic groups of students as problematic. The paradigmatic shift is from a value of "tolerating diversity" to a "transformational commitment to equity." This shift is characterized by:

- Representative comments from the "tolerance" paradigm are: Their culture doesn't value education. They just need to work harder. It isn't about race it is about socioeconomic status. They just need to pull themselves up by their bootstraps—it is the American way!
- In contrast, culturally proficient educational leaders hold a "transformational" paradigm that views their work in terms of how they affect the educational experiences of people culturally different from themselves. Transformational comments are: What do we need to learn to be effective? What might be instructional approaches that work in this setting? In what ways can I organize the agenda to focus on being solution centered?

CULTURAL PROFICIENCY AS AN EDUCATIONAL LEADERSHIP LENS

Culturally proficient educational leaders are effective in cross-cultural situations that affect their students, the communities they serve, and the educators and staff members in their schools. Culturally proficient educational leaders are committed to educating all students to high levels through knowing, valuing, and using the students' cultural backgrounds, languages, and learning styles within the selected curricular and instructional contexts. Leaders who are committed to leading our schools in a way that all students have access to the benefits of a democratic system can use the four tools of cultural proficiency as a template for their personal and professional development.

The tools of cultural proficiency provide you with:

- **guiding principles** on which you can build an ethical and professional frame for effective cross-cultural communication and problem solving
- **a continuum** of behaviors that enables you to diagnose your values and behavior in such a way that you can better influence the policies and practices of our profession

- **essential elements**, expressed in terms of standards of personal and professional conduct, that serve as a framework for intentionally responding to the academic and social needs of the cultural groups in your school and community
- **barriers** to this work framed in such a way that you are intentional in the use of the guiding principles and essential elements

Effective use of these tools is predicated on a willingness to put into operation the agreements listed above that begin with you the leader, not with those you lead. It is our experience that effective educational leaders are very clear about themselves relative to working with and leading culturally diverse communities.

THE CULTURAL PROFICIENCY TOOLKIT

Cultural proficiency is comprised of an interrelated set of four tools that prompt reflection and provide the opportunity to improve your leadership practice in service of others. The tools provide you with the means by which to lead your personal life and perform your professional responsibilities in a culturally proficient manner.

The Guiding Principles of Cultural Proficiency

The key question in considering the guiding principles is, *Is what we "say" as school leaders congruent with what we "do?"* In reflecting on your responses to the Getting Centered activity at the beginning of this chapter, did you experience dissonance between how you respond to others' inappropriate comments and how you would like to respond? Did you find disconnect between how colleagues talk about cultural groups of students and the types of comments you know to be healthier? If you pause in considering your responses to these questions, you are in the throes of an ethical dilemma.

The guiding principles provide a moral philosophical framework (Shapiro & Stefkovich, 2005) for you to examine and understand your beliefs about the education of students from cultural groups different from yours. Once you consider your own beliefs, the guiding principles will help you examine the core values of your school. Using the guiding principles will support you as you develop a coherent approach to educating all students in ways that honor and build on who they are as people and as members of our complex, often contradictory, society.

The guiding principles provide a framework for how the cultural diversity of your students should inform professional practice when responding to student learning needs. A good place to see if the stated values in your school align with predominant behaviors in the school is to examine your school or district's mission, vision, or beliefs statement. Most likely in looking at school and district mission statements you will encounter phrases such as:

- all students
- valuing diversity
- twenty-first century education
- high tech skills

Do your leadership behaviors and those of your colleagues align with those expressed values? To assist, please read the guiding principles of cultural proficiency displayed in Table 2.1. As you read the six bulleted items, pay attention to your reactions and to the questions that arise for you.

Table 2.1   The Guiding Principles of Cultural Proficiency

- Culture is a predominant force in people's and school's lives.
- People are served in varying degrees by the dominant culture.
- People have group identities and individual identities.
- Diversity within cultures is vast and significant.
- Each cultural group has unique cultural needs.
- The best of both worlds enhances the capacity of all.

Reflection

Use the space below to record your thoughts, reaction, and questions as you read Table 2.1.

_____

_____

_____

_____

The Cultural Proficiency Continuum

Table 2.2 presents the six points of the continuum with brief descriptions. First, note the manner in which the continuum is constructed:

- The first three points of the continuum focuses on *them* (i.e., your students and their culture) as being problematic. Cultural destructiveness, cultural incapacity, and cultural blindness seek to have you looking out Collins's (2001) "window" and describing students with terms such as *underperforming.*
- The next three points of the continuum focus on your *practice as transformational leadership.* Cultural precompetence, cultural competence, and cultural proficiency have you looking in Collins's "mirror" and examining your educational practices and seeking to know how you are *under serving* your students and their communities so you can learn to serve them differently (i.e., an example of the inside-out approach).

Table 2.2   Leadership and the Cultural Proficiency Continuum

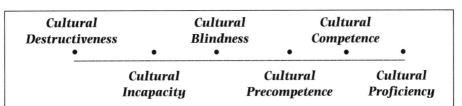

- **Cultural Destructiveness**—Leading in a manner that you seek to eliminate the cultures of others in all aspects of the school and in relationship with the community served.
- **Cultural Incapacity**—Leading in a way that you trivialize other cultures and seek to make the culture of others appear to be wrong.
- **Cultural Blindness**—Leading where you don't see or acknowledge the culture of others and you choose to ignore the discrepant experiences of cultures within the school.
- **Cultural Precompetence**—Leading with an increasing awareness of what you and the school don't know about working in diverse settings. At this level of development you and the school can move in a positive, constructive direction or you can falter, stop, and possibly regress.
- **Cultural Competence**—Leading with your personal values and behaviors and the school's policies and practices being aligned in a manner that is inclusive with cultures that are new or different from you and the school.
- **Cultural Proficiency**—Leading as an advocate for life-long learning with the purpose of being increasingly effective in serving the educational needs of cultural groups. Holding the vision that you and the school are instruments for creating a socially just democracy.

Reflection

What questions and thoughts occur to you as you read Table 2.2 and the introductory comments that precede it? Use the space below to record your thoughts, reactions, and questions.

_____

_____

_____

_____

The Five Essential Elements of Cultural Competence

The essential elements are the standards for culturally competent values, behaviors, policies, and practices. Table 2.3 presents an overview of the essential elements with leadership illustrations. Later, Chapter 7 is structured to provide you the opportunity to work in depth with these elements.

Table 2.3   The Essential Elements for Culturally Proficient Leadership

- **Assessing Cultural Knowledge**—Leading the learning about others' cultures, about how educators and the school as a whole react to others' cultures, and what you need to do to be effective in cross-cultural situations. Also, leading for learning about the school and its grade levels and departments as cultural entities.
- **Valuing Diversity**—Creating informal and formal decision-making groups inclusive of people whose viewpoints and experiences are different from yours and the dominant group at the school, and that will enrich conversations, decision making, and problem solving.
- **Managing the Dynamics of Difference**—Modeling problem solving and conflict resolution strategies as a natural and normal process within the organizational culture of the schools and the cultural contexts of the communities of your school.
- **Adapting to Diversity**—Being the lead learner at your school about cultural groups different from your own and the ability to use others' cultural experiences and backgrounds in all school settings.
- **Institutionalizing Cultural Knowledge**—Making learning about cultural groups and their experiences and perspectives an integral part of the school's professional development.

Overcoming Barriers to Cultural Proficiency

In the manner that the guiding principles provide a moral compass for culturally proficient actions, there are barriers to achieving culturally proficient actions. Table 2.4 presents three common barriers and descriptions of behaviors associated with each barrier. The barriers when present in our behaviors or the practices in our schools exist together in combination, not as isolated events.

Table 2.4   Barriers to Cultural Proficiency

- **Resistance to Change**—Many educators and schools often struggle with change that involves issues of culture. For those who are resistant, change often is experienced as an outside force that judges current practices as deficient or defective. Whether accurate or not, an adversarial relationship exists between those forcing the change and the members of the school.
- **Systems of Oppression**—That racism, sexism, heterosexism, ableism, and classism exist is without refute, historically and currently. Data are on the side of documenting and describing the ill effects of such systems. Being able to understand oppression as a systemic issue apart from personal behavior is important.
- **A Sense of Privilege and Entitlement**—Systems of oppression have two effects—on those who are harmed and on those who benefit. Those harmed from systemic oppressions respond from an emotional connection and become very knowledgeable of practices that impact them negatively. Many of those who benefit from historical and current practices are oblivious to the negative effects of systemic oppression on others because they can choose not to see.

Barriers are often manifested in statements such as these:

- It is not me that needs to change.
- I have been a successful educator for years.
- These kids/parents just need to get a clue!

Similarly, it is rare to find the person who doesn't acknowledge that racism, ethnocentrism, and sexism exist in our society; but, what they often fail to see is that when one group of people loses rights and privileges due to systemic oppression, those rights and privileges accrue to others in often unacknowledged or unrecognized ways. It is when one recognizes one's entitlement that he or she has the ability to make choices that benefit the education of children and youth.

When focusing on the achievement issues of nondominant students, most educators and educational policymakers? experience a conversation gap. The gap in conversation, which is often unrecognized and unacknowledged, is educators not having the perspective to see road-blocks that have been, and are, impeding members of nondominant socioeconomic, racial, ethnic, gender, or language groups. This selective invisibility leads to a sense of privilege and entitlement for members of the dominant group. Whereas systems of oppression impose barriers for members of nondominant groups, concomitant systems of privilege and entitlement impose barriers for members of the dominant group. The barriers erected by a sense of privilege and entitlement involve a skewed sense of reality that impedes one's ability to pursue ethical and moral avenues in meeting the academic and social needs of nondominant groups of students.

The position of privilege often fosters educators voicing biased or ill-informed assumptions about parents from nondominant groups. Typical of such assumptions are comments such as:

- Their parents won't come to parent conferences because they don't care about the education of their child.
- Why try to help them, they will just end up to be gang bangers, just like their dad!
- Why should I learn anything about their culture? This is our country; let them learn about us!

Educators who make comments like those above are in need of different lenses, tools, and structures to understand their students, the barriers they face, and the special learning needs they have in order to be successful in school. As a leader, you can use the guiding principles, the continuum, and the essential elements to frame conversations with fellow educators about how parents and students who are culturally different from them behave and learn. Cultural proficiency is:

- an approach for surfacing educators' assumptions and values that undermine the success of some student groups
- a lens for examining how we include and honor the cultures and learning needs of all students in the educational process

Reflection

How comfortable are you with your knowledge of cultural proficiency? What questions do you have? What more do you want to learn about the tools of cultural proficiency? How do you see the tools of cultural proficiency helping you lead your school in a manner that serves the academic and social needs of all cultural groups of students?

_____

_____

_____

_____

NOTE

1.   A collective and emerging term that describes indigenous people who are not Inuit or Metis—Province of Ontario, Canada. *Human rights code.*

Constructing Your Cultural Autobiography

3

Remember, you don't fear people whose stories you know.

—Margaret Wheatley (2002, p. 145)

GETTING CENTERED

This chapter provides you with the initial tools for constructing your cultural autobiography. You may have participated in similar activities prior to today or this may be your first opportunity to do so. What thoughts are with you as you begin to consider this task? What feelings and reactions are surfacing for you? Please take a few moments and record these initial thoughts, feelings, and reactions in the space below.

A premise of this book is that we are all cultural beings. Some of us are very aware of our cultural identity in terms of race, ethnicity, gender, sexual orientation, ableness, faith, and socioeconomic status. Others of us, for many reasons, either are unaware of our cultural identities or reject the importance of culture in our lives. Those of us who are unaware or who reject the importance of culture are often people so well served by current policies and practices that we view our experiences as normative and believe it is incumbent on others to *work harder, just as I have had to!* While we subscribe to the value of working hard to be important, we also realize that for many people the lack of access to opportunity is not related to how hard they work. It is for this reason that we invite you, whether fully aware of your cultural being-ness or somewhat reluctant to buy into this notion, to take this cultural journey with us.

In this chapter, you are provided opportunities to record when you first became aware of various cultural groups to which you belong. In Chapters 4–6, you will build on this information by reflecting on personal cross-cultural growth experiences you have had and then by interviewing people culturally different from you. Your reflections and your interview notes are to guide you in understanding your assumptions about people culturally different from you. As you combine the *content* of your cultural autobiography with the *context* of your reflections and interview notes, you will be engaging in the *inside-out* process that is fundamental in your journey to cultural proficiency.

YOUR CULTURAL AUTOBIOGRAPHY

Tables 3.1, 3.2, and 3.3 on pages 33, 34, and 36 are designed for you to describe your earliest awareness of six cultural groups to which you belong. Table 3.4 on page 38 provides the opportunity to describe a cultural group we have not included. Table 3.5 on page 40 guides you in reflecting on your responses and writing what you are learning about yourself.

You are encouraged to begin with any of the tables in this chapter that work best for you. There is no hierarchy or priority to the sequence of tables. The important thing is for you to be in a contemplative mood, to have time to think and reflect, and to write as thoughts occur to you. It may be that you will format these questions onto your laptop because that medium is more comfortable for your writing. Most likely you will write a little bit today, put away your writing, and later add to your writing as reflections occur to you. Most important, this is *your* work and you are encouraged to use an approach and pacing that works best for you.

To facilitate your thinking and writing, each table is introduced with a brief context statement. We want you to think deeply about the questions in each of the tables in an authentic manner that yields an emerging portrait of you as a cultural being.

Your Race/Ethnicity and Gender Cultures

Our racial, ethnic, and gender identities emerge early in life (Bochenek & Brown, 2001; Clark & Clark, 1950; Sadker & Sadker, 1994). In Table 3.1 you have the opportunity to recall your earliest remembrances of your race/ethnicity and gender. What is it about your earliest recollection of your racial or ethnic identity that you recall? Was the earliest recollection of your racial/ethnic identity associated with someone like you or with someone different from you? Was it a positive experience? Was it a negative experience? Or, was it just "an experience?" What about the experience made it memorable? Please record your responses to these and any other questions that occur to you in the top portion of Table 3.1.

Similarly, what is it about your earliest recollection of your gender identity that you recall? What people in your life contributed to your awareness of your gender identity? What kind of an experience was it for you? Please record your responses to these and any other questions that occur in the lower portion of Table 3.1.

Reflection

Take a moment and reread your entries to Table 3.1. What reactions do you have as you reread and think about your recollections? Take a few moments and write your thoughts and reactions in the space below.

_____

_____

_____

_____

Your Sexual Orientation and Social Class Cultures

Chances are pretty good that if you are a heterosexual person, you may be experiencing a visceral reaction to the topic of sexual orientation. If you are a gay, lesbian, bisexual, transgendered, or intersex person, you may have a visceral reaction, too. Whatever your orientation, raising the issue of sexual orientation has been one of the topics most avoided by the dominant culture in our schools and our society. Whether we are open or closed about our sexual orientation, the fact remains that we have such a cultural identity. Our questions are similar to those for race, ethnicity, and gender. When did you first become aware of your sexual orientation? Was your first recognition of your sexual orientation in response to those like you, or those different from you, or from some other source? Describe your

Table 3.1   My Cultural Identity—Race, Ethnicity, and Gender

Describe when you first became aware of your race and/or ethnicity.
Describe when you first became aware of your gender.

Table 3.2   My Cultural Identity—Sexual Orientation and Social Class

Describe when you first became aware of your sexual orientation.
Describe when you first became aware of your social class.

initial experience in recognizing your sexual orientation in terms of the experience being a positive, negative, or some other type of experience. Why do you think you remember the experience? Please use the upper half of Table 3.2 to record your responses.

Membership in a socioeconomic group, or social class, is often difficult for many of us. Probably the greatest number of people in our country would identify themselves as being "middle class." When recalling your first experience of recognizing your social class, what experience or image comes to mind? Was it a positive, negative, or some other type of experience? What do you remember about the experience? Why do you think you remember the experience? Please use the lower half of Table 3.2 to record your responses.

Reflection

Please reread your entries to Table 3.2. What reactions do you have as you reread and think about your recollections? Take a few moments and write your thoughts and reactions in the space below.

_____

_____

_____

_____

Your Ableness and Faith Cultures

One's ableness is another of our cultural groupings that is more apparent to some in our society than it is to others. There are some of you reading this who most likely view others as being *differently abled* when, in reality, we are all differently abled. Sit with that last sentence for a moment and think about it—when did you first recognize that *you* were differently abled than others around you? What was the experience like for you—positive, negative, or other? What is it about that experience that you remember it? Please use the upper half of Table 3.3 to record your thoughts and reactions.

One's faith is the lone category, so far in this exercise, that is somewhat of a choice when compared to the other cultural groups discussed previously. However, many of us continue, at least nominally, to adhere to the practices of our forebears. You may have retained your inherited disposition to faith, religion, and spirituality or you may have chosen a very different path for yourself. Irrespective of your current adherence and

Table 3.3   My Cultural Identity—Ableness and Faith

Describe when you first became aware of your mental and physical ableness.
Describe when you first became aware of your faith, religion, spirituality, or the absence thereof.

practice, what is your orientation to presence or absence of faith? Was the experience positive, negative, or something different for you? Please use the lower half of Table 3.3 to record your responses.

Reflection

Review your entries to Table 3.3. What reactions do you have as you reread and think about your recollections? Take a few moments and write your thoughts and reactions in the space below.

_____

_____

_____

_____

_____

_____

Other Cultural Groups

At this point you may be looking at yourself and recognizing that you have other cultural groups that are important parts of who you are and what you do. Table 3.4 is for your use to list other cultural groups and to ask yourself these questions: When did you first recognize that you were a member of the cultural group? Was this earliest recognition as a member of this cultural group associated with those who are members of this group or those not members of the group? Was the experience positive, negative, or other? What makes the experience memorable?

Reflection

Take a moment and reread your entries to Table 3.4. What reactions do you have as you reread and think about your recollections? Take a few moments and write your thoughts and reactions in the space below.

_____

_____

_____

_____

_____

_____

Table 3.4   My Cultural Identity _____

Describe when you first became aware of your cultural identity as _____.
Describe when you first became aware of your cultural identity as _____.

Synthesizing the Cultural You

The information you have entered into Tables 3.1–3.4 provides significant elements defining who you are. First, and maybe most important, it is information you gathered about yourself. As such, you may want to revisit this activity from time to time and add recollections and details that provide even deeper insight. Second, your entries are evidence that you are a cultural being. Though you are an individual with distinctive and diverse characteristics, interests, and abilities, you are also a member of several cultural groups. Individuality and cultural membership are not dichotomous.

The information you gathered in this chapter is the initial step in constructing a picture of the extent your cultural memberships have influenced who you are today—the assumptions that underlie who you are as a person. In later chapters, you will build on this information as you consider PreK–12 education and implications for you as a leader. Table 3.5 provides space for you to consider how the earliest recollections of your cultural being have influenced you. As you reread and reflect on your entries to Tables 3.1–3.4, search for themes that might influence your development as a cultural being and record your responses to questions such as these in Table 3.5:

- What is your value for people different from you or like you?
- What beliefs do you have about those who are like or different from you?
- What customs are emerging in how you respond to those different from or like you? What cross-cultural traditions, if any, endure in your life? If none, why do you think that to be?
- What is your view of the language you speak and the languages spoken by others?
- How do you view the world—as the small space around you or larger and more encompassing? How do you know?
- What assumptions do you make about those who are different from you?

In your recollections in Tables 3.1–3.4 and in identifying patterns in those recollections in Table 3.5, you are beginning the process of linking the foundations of your personal assumptions in a manner that will help you to understand yourself within the context of public education and yourself as an educational leader. Chapters 4–6 guide you in developing a framework for making intentional, equity-based choices as a school leader.

Table 3.5   My Cultural Identity—Summary of Learning

Review your responses in Tables 3.1–3.4 and summarize what you are learning about your cultural identity.

- What is your value for people different from you or like you?

- What beliefs do you have about those who are like or different from you?

- What customs are emerging in how you respond to those different from or like you?

- What cross-cultural traditions, if any, endure in your life? If none, why do you think that to be?

- What is your view of the language you speak and the languages spoken by others?

- How do you view the world—as the small space around you; or larger and more encompassing; or somewhere in between those extremes? How do you know?

- What assumptions do you make about those who are different from you?

Reflection

Writing your cultural autobiography is quite an accomplishment! What thoughts and feelings are with you right now? Please use the space below to record your responses.

_____

_____

_____

_____

Part II

Knowing Ourselves

Responding to Issues Related to Race, Ethnicity, and National Origin

4

Randy, what is it like being a white man in this country?

—Ray Terrell (circa, 1972)

GETTING CENTERED

Think of a time recently when you heard the word *racism* used to describe some aspect of education. Recall your feelings at the time. Then, think back and remember how those around you responded. How were your feelings or reactions "similar" to the people around you? How were your feelings or reactions "different" from those around you? How did you respond at the time? How did you respond later? How do you respond now? Please use the space below to respond to the questions that resonate for you.

_____

_____

_____

_____

The epigraph that leads this chapter may have been the genesis for our writing this book. The day Ray asked Randy that question in 1972, we had concluded a day of cross-cultural training with fellow educators that had been difficult. It was our experience that discussions about race were usually difficult, and engaging the discussions resulted in passionate comments on both sides of the issue. Our African American colleagues were clear about the negative effects of racism and how dominant society benefited from current practices. At the same time, many of our white colleagues, while similarly clear about the negative effects of racism, often felt blamed by the intensity of these discussions. Following one of these sessions was when Ray asked Randy the question, *What's it like to be a white man in this country?* We realized our discussions about racism centered more on its negative effects and much less on how racism benefited the dominant group.

Ray's honest curiosity led Randy into deep introspection and both of us, ultimately, to examining ourselves with reference to cultural groups different from us. As Randy became clearer on the privileges he has as a white man in this society, we both began an odyssey of self-discovery about ourselves as cultural beings. As two men, one African American and one European American, we share our cultural autobiographies, excerpted in this chapter and also Chapters 5 and 6, as illustrations of our growing awareness of cultural issues. The manners in which we wrote our autobiographies are not intended to be models or prototypes; you will want to develop an approach that serves your needs. The vignettes from our autobiographies are to illustrate how learning about embedded assumptions and values enhances one's cross-cultural effectiveness. We have had to continually push against the respective privilege and entitlement accorded to us in interacting with those culturally different from ourselves.The premise of Chapters 4–6 is that you can help introduce and facilitate productive discussions among colleagues when you are clear about who you are in relation to students' cultures (i.e., race, ethnicity, national origin, language, gender, social class, sexual orientation, ableness, or faith).

The term *undiscussables* is an apt word to describe the avoidance that too often takes place among educators in our schools and related organizations in discussions about students' cultures. For too long, topics related to race, ethnicity, national origin, as well as the topics in Chapters 5 and 6, have been rendered invisible in educators' discussions. With this book it is our intent to take topics that have been invisible and undiscussable to become visible and part of the every day conversation among educators. Our objective is for you and your colleagues to experience students' cultures as natural and normal topics for discussion free of anger, guilt, and blame. When you have explicit agreements about the presence and impact of culture, the current accountability movement and its use of disaggregated data becomes an indispensable ally. In such a context, discussions about students' disparate success in issues of curriculum, assessment, and access to higher-order thinking experiences become natural and normal.

As you now know, it is our belief that the first step in this process begins *within* each of us. In this chapter you have the opportunity to explore prior experiences with issues arising from race, ethnicity, and national origin and to interview and interact with people different from you. The desired outcome of this activity and the related activities in Chapters 5 and 6 is for you to know more deeply the basis of your assumptions about those different from you and to be intentional in future interactions with people culturally different from you.

RAY AND RANDY'S DISCLAIMER: OUR EMERGENT AWARENESS OF "ISMS"

We have organized Chapters 4–6 in the sequence that cultural issues unfolded for us in our careers. In this chapter we discuss issues related to race, ethnicity, and national origin. Chapter 5 introduces the topics of language acquisition, gender, and social class. Chapter 6 covers the topics of sexual orientation, faith, and ableness. The topics could have been organized in many different ways; the unfolding of the issues has not been linear in our lives and represents the approximate sequence we began to see them as part of overall systemic oppression.

HISTORICAL CONTEXT: RACE, ETHNICITY, AND NATIONAL ORIGIN

Federal and state reform mandates such as No Child Left Behind (2002) highlight disparities in student achievement and, concomitantly, related discussions often uncover negative feelings and attitudes that challenge the most skilled educational leader. We believe this difficulty rests on two pillars—issues of race and racism in this country are unresolved; and, such discussions raise emotions on both sides of the debate and cloud rational discussion.

Educators receive children and youth into their classrooms and schools who are impacted by many historical forces. As teachers, counselors, and administrators it becomes our responsibility, in addition to being competent in our academic educator role, to expand that academic role to include competence in understanding the impact of identified historical and social forces on our students. Issues of racism, ethnocentrism, and segregation generationally impeded access to the material benefits of society. These issues are the "back story" of access and achievement gaps. The historical nature and persistence of access and achievement gaps provide the impetus for current state and national initiatives for school reform in ways that acknowledge and confront disparate achievement among demographic groups of students. Jack O'Connell, California's Superintendent of Public Instruction, is one of the most prominent elected politicians to acknowledge the racial correlates for educational gaps. Responding to the lagging achievement scores of black and Latino students, the *Los Angeles Times* reported:

> "These are not just economic achievement gaps, they are racial achievement gaps," O'Connell said after his annual release of California's standardized test scores. "We cannot afford to excuse them; they simply must be addressed." (Landsberg & Blume, 2007)

It would be easy to speak of Mr. O'Connell's pronouncement as "courageous," however we welcome this "appropriate" statement as long overdue in our country. Mr. O'Connell is providing responsible leadership to the public schools of California and trusting that his colleagues in the other forty-nine states, if they hadn't already discovered the link between race and achievement, will soon join him. Mr. O'Connell followed his public pronouncement by sponsoring a statewide educational summit in which over 4,000 attendees publicly addressed the issue of race and access and achievement gaps. Following Mr. O'Connell's initiative, the Association of California School Administrators has moved this topic to its annual preconference agenda for 2008.

Our intent in the section that follows is to present to you some of the historically based social and political forces that continue to impact our PreK–12 schools. This book is not presented as a U.S. History, contemporary sociology, or curriculum and instruction text. There are many excellent texts that present detailed descriptions and cogent rationales for multicultural education in its many forms (Banks, 1999; Gollnick & Chinn, 2006; Sleeter & Grant, 2007). Similarly, Takaki (1989, 1993), Handlin (1954), McWilliams (1968), Franklin and Moss (1988), Brown (1971), Deloria (1969), Acuna (1987), Galarza (1971), and Sadker and Sadker (1994) are among the many scholars who have dedicated their careers to documenting and describing both the contributions made by different cultural groups to the fabric that is our country as well as the often horrific barriers constructed to impede their progress. We commend each of these texts for use in your continued personal and professional development.

Our National History of Racism and Ethnocentrism

Often at the beginning of our professional development sessions on cultural proficiency, we present a consideration to our audiences that almost always elicits seemingly befuddled amusement—*Please raise your hand if you think racism has existed in the history of our country.* Virtually all participants raise their hands, sometimes slowly, as if to wonder what question will follow. And, our next consideration is, *Please raise your hands if you believe vestiges of racism persist in today's society.* Again, virtually all hands are raised. Having repeated this exercise with teachers, counselors, administrators, educators in California, and educators across the United States and Canada, we have come to the conclusion that there is little doubt in the minds of most educators that racism exists. When we get "push back" about racism, the most common response becomes, "When these groups assimilate into the dominant culture, disparities will no longer exist." It is not difficult to understand this perspective, whether one embraces it or not, because European Americans have often assimilated into the dominant culture within three generations (Takaki, 1993). Assimilation is often accompanied by the "boot straps" analogy used by many dominant group spokespeople who believe their forebears' experiences were typical of all who came to these shores. Race was, in fact, the basis for experiences that were horribly different in quantum proportions. In stark contrast to the historical assimilation of European Americans has been the systematic genocide, domination, and exclusion visited on First Nation Peoples and African Americans. These historically different experiences among cultural groups gave rise to segregation and, ultimately, the legal and moral press for desegregation and integration.

One of the legacies of racism has been the pitting of lower socioeconomic white people against people of color. In rural and urban locales across the country, racism is exacerbated when people compete for scacre resources or the perception of scarce resources. Historically, in the urban centers of the north, the rural sectors of the south, and the agricultural regions of the west, lower socioeconomic whites have repressed African Americans, Mexican Americans and First Nations People. These behaviors continue to contribute to spiraling racism and prejudice. Acts of prejudice and racism were institutionalized into neighborhood covenants that limited occupancy to white people, to discriminatory hiring practices in companies of all sizes, and by politicians who routinely conjure up images of menacing African Americans, Mexican Americans, and Native Americans to control elections. It is the vestiges of these visions of white entitlement that cause poor white people to act in discriminatory and hostile ways. The unfortunate by-product of this faux entitlement is that both groups continue to be marginalized in the job market, in the political world, and in our schools.

Segregation, Desegregation, and Integration

Since the 1970s, schools have been moved from legally segregated to desegregated, if not integrated, and often resegregated sites. Those of you who were not educators at the time were, quite possibly, students during such experiences. Desegregation has taken many forms—mandatory plans that often included busing students from home neighborhoods, boundary changes that involved students attending schools in other neighborhoods, and voluntary plans that are usually organized around an educational theme such as technology or the arts. In each of these forms, desegregation was intended to reduce the harmful effects of racial isolation and to provide historically segregated students access to the material and human resources of students better served by our educational systems. The very existence of the various historical and current approaches to school attendance boundaries and patterns are testimony to a history of inequity. Whether African American, Mexican American, or First Nations, students in *de jure* school systems (i.e., segregated-by-law) throughout the U.S. or in *de facto* segregated schools (i.e., segregation-in-fact though without legal basis), it is indisputable that our school systems still fail to educate all of our students comparably.

Using the language of cultural proficiency, *de jure segregation* is an explicit example of cultural destructiveness. The overt separation of students by race and gender (i.e., cultural destructiveness) was intended to maintain benefits for white and male students, respectively, while repressing opportunities and access for students of color and women. *De facto segregation* is a clear example of cultural incapacity and cultural blindness. Differential access to high quality education dependent on neighborhood or zip code is for all intents and purposes segregation; however, the term *de facto* is modified. Whether we identify "those schools" as inferior due to their demographic composition (i.e., cultural incapacity) or we pretend not to see the disparities among schools and school districts (i.e., cultural blindness), the negative consequence of lack of access to high quality education is the same.

Social, Economic, and Political Forces Impinge on Schooling

Schools exist within a social, economic, and political context. Social forces such as disparities in access to health care and unemployment rates, economic forces such as discrimination in housing and disparities in wages, and gerrymandering to preserve dominant group political influence are well documented practices that affect schooling (Berliner, 2005; Kozol, 2007). Common refrains from fellow educators when discussing disparities are:

- "What can we do? These issues are much bigger than what I can impact."
- "No wonder these kids can't achieve; have you seen their neighborhoods?"
- "Given the environment these kids live in, we can't put pressure on them to be as academically successful as their counterparts in successful schools. It is just not fair to them!"

And, of course the often used refrain:

- "They are doing the best they can."

It would be a mistake to say that progress and impediments to student achievement are the sole provinces of educational systems when outside forces do affect our students. However, it is disingenuous to abdicate our responsibility to these very real outside forces in closing these educational gaps, too. To come to grips with these seemingly contrasting perspectives is to avoid the trap of dichotomizing the social forces that impinge on our schools from our responsibilities as educators. In truth, education must not be an "either-or" experience and we do have the ethical and moral responsibility to do all that we can to educate our students.

Our educational systems have been touted as the avenue by which people access the benefits of our democratic society. For European immigrants in the late nineteenth and early twentieth century, in particular, that avenue has worked within two to three generations as they became Americans (Takaki, 1993). Even though generational poverty remains a persistent force affecting large numbers of white citizens, poverty combined with racism and ethnocentrism have impacted African Americans, First Nations People, and Latinos in ways that continue the legacies of segregation in more modern *de facto* ways of isolating students in underresourced schools. Most of our schools, whether urban or rural, identified as chronically "underperforming" also have much higher turnover rates of experienced teachers, dilapidated facilities, and overcrowded classrooms than do schools where students are academically more successful (Lindsey et al., 2008). The achievement gap that persists is one such artifact of the legacy of segregation.

Reflection

Take a moment and think of your school and its demographic composition by race, ethnicity, and national origin? What opportunities exist in everyday interactions for faculty and students to get to know people from other racial or ethnic groups? Where in the school's curricula do students learn about other cultural groups? What forces within your school promote cross-cultural learning? What forces inhibit or impede cross-cultural learning? Please write your responses in the space below.

_____

_____

_____

_____

The Achievement Gap Is a Test of our Moral Bearing

National Assessment of Educational Progress (NAEP) testing (Perie, Moran, & Lutkus, 2005) identified the achievement gap in clear, unambiguous terms. However, it took federal legislation, No Child Left Behind (NCLB) (2002), and similar state initiatives to mandate that we educators address the disparities in educational achievement. Today the achievement gaps persist within the context of gains being reported in reading and mathematics for all demographic groups (Perie et al., 2005).The identification of disparate student achievement recorded by demographic groups of students is a significant outcome of the assessment and accountability movement given impetus by NCLB and the various state reform initiatives. Race, ethnicity, and national origin are now visible and members of these groups need to be served differently. In Chapter 5 we address three more groups made visible—language, gender, and socioeconomic status. Chapter 6 addresses sexual orientation, faith, and ableness. While our current accountability systems have made ableness more visible, sexual orientation and faith are not accorded visibility status in most of our schools.

Let us be clear. As authors who have been working with these issues for over forty years, we do not believe that standardized tests measure the only impact that schools can and should have on students. However, we believe that tests such as NAEP are an appropriate barometer for who is and who is not being well served in our schools. Our responsibility as school leaders is to provide a vision inclusive of the academic and social needs of all students. In Chapter 2, we described the tools of cultural proficiency as a framework for individual educators and school communities to address disparities in access and achievement. The fourth tool of cultural proficiency detailed in Chapter 2 describes the process of recognizing and overcoming self-imposed and institutional barriers to cultural proficiency. Self-imposed barriers are the assumptions and filters used to make invisible the disparities that exist in our schools. Whether we disaggregate student achievement data or analyze data regarding student access to higher-order learning experiences, data exists to shed light on who is and who is not being well served in our schools. Institutional barriers include policies and practices that channel students into programs and experiences aligned with their cultural groups and result in underrepresentation of African American and First Nations students in honors and advanced placement programs and overrepresentation of these same groups in mild to moderate special education programs.

Educators engaged in the journey to cultural proficiency learn of the impact their expectations have on all students. Our expectations shape the culture of the school and schooling in ways that facilitate or impede the learning of students of color. The culturally proficient educator expands her repertoire of individual values and behaviors and her school's policies and practices to be inclusive of students' cultures in ways that facilitate learning. The cultural proficiency continuum provides a framework for seeing and understanding educators' values and behavior and the school's policies and practices.

THE CULTURAL PROFICIENCY CONTINUUM:
A GUIDE FOR YOUR REFLECTIONS

The cultural proficiency continuum provides language to describe unhealthy and healthy *values and behaviors* of persons and *policies and practices* of organizations. As you construct your responses to the prompts in this and later chapters, you may find yourself turning back to the continuum to aid you in recognizing and understanding your values and behaviors and your school's policies and practices.

If you need to review the continuum, please turn back to Chapter 2 of this book to familiarize yourself with the continuum as one of the tools of cultural proficiency. For our purposes in this and the chapters to follow, movement along the continuum represents a shift in thinking from holding the view of *tolerating diversity* to *transformation for equity*. It is our experience that this is not a subtle shift in worldview; for many people, it is paradigmatic. The shift in thinking occurs when we cease blaming our students, their culture, their parents, or their neighborhoods for lack of success in schools and, instead, engage in examining our current educational practices and changing them when necessary to respond to the educational needs and learning styles of our students. As you read vignettes from our cultural autobiographies and construct your own recollections and reflections, please use the continuum as a frequent reference point to gauge your and your school's resistance, regression, learning, and progress that each of us make to be effective in our diverse society.

The continuum can be readily organized into two phases, each of which presents a contrasting view of how you might interact with groups different from you (see Table 4.1). To the left side of the continuum are personal values and behaviors or institutional policies and practices that, at best, *tolerate diversity:*

- Cultural Destructiveness—you or your school seek to eliminate vestiges of the cultures of others.
- Cultural Incapacity—you or your school seek to make the culture of others appear to be wrong.
- Cultural Blindness—you or your school refuse to acknowledge the culture of others.

Table 4.1   The Cultural Proficiency Continuum: A Guide for Your Reflections

Cultural Destructiveness		Cultural Blindness		Cultural Competence	
	Cultural Incapacity		Cultural Precompetence		Cultural Proficiency

In contrast, to the right side of the continuum are personal values and behaviors or institutional policies and practices that seek to *transform for equity:*

- Cultural Precompetence—you or your school have a beginning awareness that current practice doesn't serve all students equitably. This can be a *breakthrough* phase in development where you become aware that you and your school can move in positive, constructive directions. However, sometimes we experience that some falter in the face of the momentousness of the changes to be made and regress to the earlier phases of cultural blindness, incapacity, or destructiveness.
- Cultural Competence—your personal and professional work is an interactive arrangement in which you and your colleagues respond to diverse settings in a manner that is additive to cultures that are different from yours.
- Cultural Proficiency—you and your colleagues make the commitment to life-long learning for the purpose of being increasingly effective in serving the educational needs of cultural groups. There is a strong sense of social justice accompanied by a demonstrated commitment to advocacy for doing what is right for our students and the communities they represent.

In writing this book we reflected on our cultural experiences and the manner in which we have evolved and continue to grow as individuals and as educators. Following are excerpts from our cultural autobiographies that we include as illustrations of our journeys of discovery. Please read our entries as illustrations, and not as prescriptions. Your journey will be different. Following our vignettes are opportunities for you to expand your cultural learning through interview and reflections. Our full cultural autobiographies are in the Appendix and, please know, they are *works in progress.*

RAY'S VIGNETTES—ONE PERSON'S EXPERIENCES

As an African American male maturing in the 1950s in Cincinnati, Ohio, I was quite clear of the opportunities and limitations provided in my community. This vignette entails two or three experiences that served, on the one hand, to develop my strength of character and, on the other hand, to make me fully aware of the societal barriers that were firmly entrenched in our society. Please read my personal experiences in a way that allows you to see and feel the everyday barriers that existed then.

The fact that my parents worked two very different jobs afforded them very different social perspectives and worldviews, and both of them freely shared their perspectives with me. As a domestic for a powerful family in the community, my mom viewed the world as a very dangerous place for African American males. She constantly admonished me to be sure to be polite and show deference to white people in order to avoid confrontations that could ultimately prove to be deadly. There was no one at my father's work place that had any community connections. He felt that he had a social responsibility to challenge the status quo around issues of social justice and constantly challenged the segregated school setting and other forms of local discrimination.

. . . .

There was another school in the village. We called it the Congress Avenue School. It served as the first twelfth grade school for white residents. The Negroes who made it to high school also attended the high school portion of the Congress Avenue School. The above reference to those "who made it" to the high school refers to the fact that the Eckstein School, the school for Negroes in Glendale, served a highly sophisticated function of sorting and determining who would get passage to move on to Glendale High School. The clear indicators of this process were marked by the number of my sixth grade classmates who were fifteen, sixteen, and even seventeen years old, and a process of repeated retention until some simply dropped out. In fact, there was a practice implemented in my seventh/eighth grade classroom where the principal, who lived in the house next-door to the school, would call roll in the morning and assign domestic work and yard work to half of my class and indicate that they would be pursuing careers as domestics and yard boys in the near future and needed to hone those skills. The rest of us would remain and engage in academic pursuits.

. . . .

It was at the hospital that I experienced my most shocking two experiences with racism and again one experience that gave me hope of redemption and kept me from painting all whites as my enemy. The first incident occurred when I was pulling duty in the emergency room. An African American male arrived in an ambulance and he was pronounced dead on arrival. I discovered that he had slipped under a railroad car at the local train station and his leg had been severed. He was initially taken to two local hospitals and been refused admission because he was black. The ambulance driver eventually brought him to the naval hospital, but too late; he had bled to death. I had never experienced anyone who had lost their life just because they were black.

. . . .

My situation became even more problematic a week later. My regular assignment was in the hospital laboratory. One night while standing watch I was called at 2:00 in the morning to go and draw blood and do a type and cross match to set up a transfusion for a white, female dependent who had just given birth and lost a lot of

(Continued)

(Continued)

blood in the process. I completed my task and the next morning I was called into the office of the hospital administrator. He informed me that the woman whose blood I had drawn had accused me of raping her while I was in the room alone with her. I was devastated and totally petrified with fear. I knew of no circumstance where such a charge when made by a white woman against an African American had ever been disbelieved, especially when there were no witnesses present. The doctor, who served as the director of the laboratory and my immediate boss, spoke and said, "The charges are bullshit." The administrator asked the doctor if an investigation had been completed? The doctor said, "No, and we aren't going to do one. I know this man well enough to know that he is not capable of such an act."

I had never had a white male step up and defend me unconditionally before. I had now experienced an all-time low and a major spiritual pick-me-up in a very short period of time. However, I still was not about to be open and trusting around white people again. Life and death based on racism became a real possibility in my life space. It was no longer something that I read about or heard people discuss. What I failed to realize even as an eighteen-year-old, was how permanent this reality would become as it continued to raise its ugly head again and again across my lifetime, up to and including this very day. What I also failed to realize was how my reality was to be so poorly understood, dismissed, and often distorted by many whites that I encountered. I began to realize that simply being white carried with it some fundamental privileges that I as an African American male would never experience, and how important my constant awareness of the color of my skin was to day-to-day emotional, psychological, and physical health and sanity.

As you finished reading this part of my story, did you picture students in your school today that may have similar experiences in their homes, schools, or communities? If so, what might be their stories? In the next section, you will be able to read the story of my friend and colleague Randy. Please note his experiences being from a lower socioeconomic strata than was mine and in being a white person.

RANDY'S VIGNETTES—ANOTHER PERSON'S EXPERIENCES

As a white male growing up in small-town middle America, I was aware of the racial attitudes of both my immediate and extended families. These vignettes portray our families as hard working, blue-collar people who, in many cases, were in a lower income social class but who harbored deep dislike for people who were different. In this case, the difference is race but it could have been any one of the other cultural groups to be covered in Chapters 5 and 6.

My first recollection of race was as a small child. I lived with my parents in a shot-gun-style house that was located on the "other side" of the railroad tracks, behind a factory, in a neighborhood that was racially mixed. We were white, and there were three groups we now call demographic groups—our labels were "colored people," the Irish, and we "Appalachians." The period was the late 1940s and early 1950s. The black men and the hillbilly men worked in one of the three factories in town... We all lived in this largely unimproved neighborhood... I never regarded it as a hard life because it wasn't. That was our life. Our house was clean and neat and I assumed that was the case for all the other families in our neighborhood.

The odd thing was that we did very little visiting with those who were not like us.

• •

The period was the mid to late 1950s. The modern civil rights movement was emerging. The Brown *decision had rolled across the country like a veritable steam-roller. In my community of marginalized, poor white people it raised all kinds of anger. I remember going to get my hair cut in Kewanee and having the barber say, "Well, if I have to cut 'their' hair, I have separate combs and brushes and I will burn them after they leave!"*

• •

In the summer of 1966 I began my Master's degree in Teaching of History at the University of Illinois where I took eight units in Negro American history. It was those eight units that formally changed my life forever. In one of the courses, I read all of the published works of James Baldwin and his novel, Another Country, has become the metaphor for my life. EVERYTHING I LEARNED WAS NEW! I already had one degree in U.S. History, but nothing I learned at the U of I was a repeat. Not even an allusion! It was all new. I was learning the history of a different United States. This was one of my first lessons in multiple perspectives!

I have learned in the ensuing decades that feelings and attitudes such as those described above are not unique to people from the southern states of the U.S. or people from lower socioeconomic groups. The dynamics of privilege and entitlement are the foundational barriers to providing an equitable school experience for all students. Resistance to school desegregation in the 1970s and 1980s that continues to persist, resistance to the development and use of curriculum and instruction programs that build on the knowledge and experiences of students, and resistance to addressing achievement gap issues as flaws in our educational processes—these are all harbingers of the maintenance of systemic privilege and entitlements that favor some within our society while ignoring or failing to meet the needs of others.

YOUR PERSONAL EXPERIENCES WITH
RACE, ETHNICITY, AND NATIONAL ORIGIN

As an educational leader, you work with people from many different cultures. In this section, we invite you to focus on your awareness of cultural differences that are of racial, ethnic, or national origin. Earlier in this chapter you read the brief historical overview of past and present practices that have as their legacies many of the disparities in our society and schools.

Table 4.2 provides you an opportunity to reflect on a personal experience in your life that contributed to your knowledge and skills of working with racial, ethnic, or national origin groups different from you. It may be that the personal experience you choose to reflect on and describe is positive or negative for you and for the other person/people involved. The purpose of this activity is for you to construct a profile of the events in your life that have contributed to the development of your attitudes, values, and behaviors regarding issues of race, ethnicity, and national origin. As you continue this journey of understanding your own personal development, you will be even better equipped to understand how the development and implementation of school policies and practices are also shaped in large part by our past experiences.

Now that you have had the opportunity to reflect on a past experience with someone who was different from you in race, ethnicity, or national origin, we challenge you to extend your personal learning journey by conducting a cultural interview.

Your Cultural Interview

You may consider the word *challenge* in the previous paragraph to be an interesting choice of terms. We use the term *challenge* at this point in the chapter with thoughtful intentionality. It is our experience that, too often, cross-cultural experiences are viewed as learning about *them—those who are different from us.* As you now know, this book is designed as a personal journey *inward*—it is about *you* learning about *you* as a person, as an educator, and as a leader in cross-cultural situations. To that end, the cultural interview protocol set forth in Table 4.3 on page 60 provides you the opportunity to extend yourself to learn about someone from a racial, ethnic, or national origin group different from you. The interview summary sheet in Table 4.4 on page 61 is for you to summarize your notes from the interview in a manner that you can analyze for themes and trends in the interview.

- Three caveats are necessary for you to know prior to conducting the cultural interview, whether the one from Table 4.3 or the corresponding interview opportunities provided in Chapters 5 and 6. First, the value of the interview is to learn about the person being interviewed.

Table 4.2   My Personal Experience

Race, Ethnicity, and National Origin

My personal growth experience with someone who is from a race, ethnicity, or national origin group different from me. Briefly, these are my three experiences:

- We were from different races -

- We were from different ethnic groups -

- We were from different national origin groups -

What I did or my response to the experiences:

- The race experience -

- The ethnicity experience -

- The national origin experience -

What might I do the next time I encounter people different from me:

- The race experience -

- The ethnicity experience -

- The national origin experience -

My lessons learned are . . .

Table 4.3   Cultural Interview

Race, Ethnicity, and National Origin

1. How do you define yourself in terms of race, ethnicity, or national origin?

2. How do you describe the structure of your family as you were growing up?

3. What is the primary language spoken in your home?

4. How do you *describe* the primary language spoken in your home?

5. How might you describe your views regarding the importance or purpose of education?

6. How might you describe customs you follow that are not reinforced in our schools?

7. How might you describe the importance of faith, religion, or spirituality in your family?

8. How might you describe your views of racial, ethnic or national origin to people different from you?

9. How might you describe people of a sexual orientation different from you?

10. How might you describe gender roles in your family?

11. How might you describe your worldview (e.g., purpose of life)?

12. What is there about you and members of your cultural group that you believe to be important but were not asked by me?

Table 4.4   Cultural Interview Summary Sheet

Race, Ethnicity, and National Origin
Now that you have interviewed a person from a racial, ethnic, or national origin group different from yours, describe how this person is different from and similar to you in terms of their:
Values
Beliefs
Customs
Traditions
Language
Worldview
What assumptions about people who are racially, ethnically, or from a national origin group different from yours were challenged as a result of this interview?

- Second, you will learn about your reactions to the material learned.
- Third, your interview with this person should not be construed as to applying to all other people of their same cultural group.

As you may recall from the description of the guiding principles of cultural proficiency in Chapter 2, there is as much diversity within cultures as there is among cultures. So, proceed with the knowledge that this is another step in your personal journey of cross-cultural learning.

Return to Your Cultural Autobiography

Take a few moments and think about all you have done in this chapter. You have read about issues that arise from race, ethnicity, and national origin differences. You have had the opportunity to reflect on past experiences, to interview people different from you, and to synthesize that information. You may find it worthwhile to return to the cultural autobiography you began in Chapter 3 and to add and modify it accordingly given the new information. Please remember that a cultural autobiography is a dynamic document that grows with your willingness to probe your inner being.

Where Are You on the Continuum?

Review your Personal Experience and Interview notes. Where do you place yourself on the cultural proficiency continuum relative to race, ethnicity, and national origin? What feelings are being generated at this point in your "inside-out" journey?

_____

_____

_____

_____

For Further Reading

The following books are recommended both for your personal reading and for use with book studies with your colleagues. The recommended books are representative of the many fine works available for professional development:

Takaki, Ronald. (1993). *A different mirror: A history of multicultural america.* Boston: Little, Brown and Company.

Gollnick, Donna M., & Chinn, Philip C. (2006). *Multicultural education in a pluralistic society.* Philadelphia: Wharton School Publishing, Pearson.

Responding to Issues Related to Language, Gender, and Social Class

5

. . . poverty has its roots in a history of racial discrimination, which cut off generations from the opportunity of America . . .

—President George W. Bush (*North County Times*, 2005)

GETTING CENTERED

Your school or school district provides recurring opportunities to engage colleagues in discussions related to students' primary language, gender, and social class. Think of a recent meeting—faculty, department/grade level, or professional development—where the topic included references to students by their primary language, gender, and/or social class. Recall how the speaker introduced the topic. Describe the speaker's demeanor while presenting the language, gender, or social class related issue. How did your colleagues react to the topic? What was your reaction? What did you *not* say at that meeting that you wish you had said? Please use the space below to write your response to these questions.

_____

_____

_____

_____

Educator discussions about student access and success in the context of students' primary language, gender, and social class are no less difficult than discussions involving students' race, ethnicity, or national origin. Again, making *undiscussables* such as language, gender, and social class visible topics for discussion is needed in many of our schools. Fortunately, we know that challenging discussions can be facilitated when key participants have knowledge of the historical context of discrimination, governmental actions to overcome discriminatory practices, and the discussion leaders' own moral centeredness for the education of all students. This chapter builds on the information from Chapter 4 by making visible issues of language acquisition, gender, and social class so they become part of our normal conversations about student access and success.

Providing equitable educational opportunities to English learner, female, and low-income students has been an ongoing struggle for the past fifty years. The 1964 Civil Rights Act (as cited in Townley & Schmeider-Ramirez, 2007), Title IX, Education Amendments 1972 (as cited in Sadker & Sadker, 1994), and *Lau v. Nichols* (1974; as cited in Nieto, 2004) expressly prohibit discrimination in educational institutions based on national origin, English learner, and gender.

The intent of this chapter, as with the previous chapter and the chapter that follows, is to provide you with the moral centeredness to take the initiative to confront the *undiscussables* by making them normal and every day topics of discussion. The undiscussables in this chapter are language, gender, and social class.

HISTORICAL CONTEXT: LANGUAGE, GENDER, AND SOCIAL CLASS

The general lack of awareness among many of our educator colleagues regarding the legal action necessary in the United States and Canada to guarantee access to education for language minority, female, and lower socioeconomic students is always disquieting.

We have taught graduate level education courses and conducted professional development sessions in schools and school districts across North America for over thirty years. We are always surprised by how many educators are not aware it took action by the U.S. Congress and the U.S. Supreme Court to guarantee access to educational resources. However, when we ask these same folks to carefully examine data from their own school or school district, they find disparities based on students' primary language, gender, and socioeconomic status. Helping fellow educators make connections between historical inequity and current access and achievement gaps builds their confidence in working with students culturally different from themselves. It is in these moments that we experience our colleagues' willingness to examine their own often unrecognized assumptions about students culturally different from them.

To augment the information presented in this chapter, you may want to consult some of the many excellent texts that present detailed descriptions and cogent rationales for inclusive education with regard to language acquisition (Cummins, 1988; Krashen, 1987; Trumbull, Rothstein-Fisch, Greenfield, & Quiroz, 2001); gender (Gilligan, 1983; Sadker & Sadker, 1994); and, social class (Zinn, 2003). These texts can serve as resources for your own continued personal and professional development and your school's book studies.

Language Acquisition

The lesson to be gained in this section is an appreciation for the reality that societal reactions and responses to language acquisition have complex, historical precedents. Our interest is for you to know about the historical dynamics of language acquisition, and to articulate and understand your reactions and responses to issues relative to language acquisition.

Language acquisition in our country has a tangled history tied to social class and the reality of some languages being valued more than others. From the very founding of our country, the educated elite have valued learning selected European languages in addition to mastery of the English language. Value for these selected languages is reflected in foreign language course offerings that continue in our schools today. Concurrent with the value for learning selected European languages has been the general societal expectation that immigrants will learn English in order to serve as functioning participants in the economic, political, and social institutions of this country. In most cases, immigrants to this country from Eastern and Southern European, Asian, and Latin American countries have been expected to learn English. Instruction in their native languages was rarely offered in U.S. schools.

English has been the language of government since our country's founding; however, it has not been the exclusive language within our country. From the very beginning of our country and continuing today, cultural communities conduct matters of business and daily life in their native languages. Even within this context of multiplicity of languages and the relative geographical isolation from Europe and Asia in the nineteenth and early twentieth centuries, English emerged as the language of commerce in the United States. While initial waves of immigrants clung to their native languages, subsequent generations learned English in order to participate fully in the society.

During the period of relative isolation in the mid-nineteenth and throughout the twentieth centuries, educated European and Asian immigrants maintained their home languages while learning English. However, even within the general expectation that immigrants learn

English, many communities in the late nineteenth century established schools in students' native European languages. In the same way we have reaction to teaching students learning in their native languages, the nineteenth century witnessed the major political parties being influenced by nativist groups collectively called "Know Nothings" that influenced political platforms to be anti-immigrant and English only (Loewen, 1995).

Language acquisition has emerged as an issue in today's schools due in large part to the mobility patterns of the late twentieth and early twenty-first centuries, the rate of undocumented immigration to the United States, and our increased involvement in interconnected economic and political cross-border arrangements. On one hand, undocumented immigration within the United States has often pitted bilingual education and English as Second Language supporters against English-only advocates. On the other hand, businesses from local owner operated to multinational corporations realize the need for employees with cross-cultural understanding and facility in languages in addition to English. Each of these realities becomes an often-competing issue for many educators in trying to address the language needs of English learners and the strident views of English only advocates.

Modern societal and educator response to issues of language acquisition has several facets. Upper middle class and upper class communities have valued learning languages in addition to English and insuring those values translated into high school course offerings. During the twentieth century, it was rare if the school did not offer Latin, French, and/or German. By the mid-twentieth century, dual immersion language programs in French, Spanish, and Japanese dotted the educational landscape. These programs were designed to preserve the cultures associated with the languages and to promote the simultaneous development of foreign language skills.

The *Lau v. Nichols* (1974; as cited in Nieto, 2004) class action law suit and the subsequent U.S. Supreme Court decision helped broaden the 1964 Civil Rights Act by holding that students in our schools with little or no facility in English should not be subjected to "sink or swim" programs and their instruction was to include instruction in one's home language. In this case, non-English speaking Chinese students held that the San Francisco School District was engaged in unequal educational opportunities. The *Lau* decision gave rise to the implementation of bilingual education, English as Second Language programs, as well as provided impetus for the "standards movement." Most important, the Supreme Court decision drew attention and mixed reaction for schools to successfully teach children from varied cultural backgrounds.

Maybe the most lasting effect of the *Lau* decision for PreK–12 educators has been the polarizing effect of language acquisition both within our profession and in society in general. Reaction to the *Lau* decision ranged from embracing the decision as an opportunity to provide equal education opportunities to fierce resistance often based in nativist reactions to immigrant groups. For experienced educators, the *Lau* decision mandated participating in university sponsored programs to augment their previously earned teaching credentials. While some educators were willing participants in earning these new "authorizations" to teach English learners, many were openly hostile to having to return to universities and further qualify their credentials. Voter reaction to bilingual programs in several states effectively ended mandatory bilingual programs in favor of programs that immersed students into English language learning.

Language acquisition, as with the other cultural issues discussed in this book, exists in combination with issues of race, ethnicity, national origin, and gender, not in immutable isolation one from another. The anti-immigrant backlash that currently sweeps the country has precedents throughout U.S. history and is focused on the newest arrivals. The anti-immigrant fervor of this early part of the twenty-first century is significant in that it is an extension of anti-Latino (mostly anti-Mexican) sentiments fostered since the late nineteenth century. In modern times, McWilliams (1968), Galarza (1971), and Carter (1970) chronicled the political, economic, and educational neglect directed toward Mexican Americans. The confluence of reactions to ethnic groups and approaches to language acquisition in our schools makes it difficult to separate ethnocentrism from discussions about language acquisition.

The legacy of the *Lau* decision and the reactions that followed may be the recognition that our schools were not serving all students equitably. When coupled with the mandates from NCLB, at minimum, we in education should be fully aware that issues of language acquisition are present in our schools and must be addressed. For example, an aspect of language acquisition too often overlooked is the education of speakers of Ebonics, Appalachian dialects, and other forms identified as "not standard English."

I, Ray, whose first language is Ebonics, struggled with learning standard English because the Ebonics form of English that I spoke was simply viewed as a misuse of standard English. The constant corrective approach left me confused. I did not need to be corrected but to be taught translation. The Ebonics that I spoke was a legitimate form of the English language. Attempting to correct me was a constant assault on my culture. When I tried to conform and speak school English, I paid a price in the community of family and friends who saw me getting above my raising because I began to talk like "white folks." In the absence of a *Lau* decision for those who speak other languages not officially classified as "foreign languages," we educators need to be aware of approaching the teaching of standard English by using Teachers of English to Speakers of Other Languages (TESOL) pedagogy of translation rather than making corrections.

Reflection

When you think of English learners in your school, what images emerge for you? When colleagues at your school or school district discuss educational issues that face English learners, how would you characterize the discussions? How do you react to the information in this section? Please enter your responses in the space provided.

_____

_____

_____

_____

Gender Issues

Issues related to gender discrimination are as old as our schools themselves. Girls and women have been systematically discriminated against since the founding of our public schools in the nineteenth century. Whether issues involved lack of access to science and mathematics courses, being counseled into "women's careers," or the glass ceiling experienced by women educators, the legacy of gender discrimination is both historical and current. Like the other issues presented in this book, those in control of our schools tried to keep gender discrimination and sexism as an "undiscussable." Fortunately, current accountability systems spawned by NCLB and state-level school reform initiatives have made disparities in achievement a gender-based visible issue.

Early in our careers as school desegregation specialists in the Princeton City School District (Cincinnati, Ohio) and the Kankakee (Illinois) School District, we had the opportunity to participate in a seminar with two young scholars from American University, Myra and David Sadker. The Sadkers had emerged as the foremost voices in studying discrimination against girls in our PreK–12 schools. Their research ranged from gender representation in curriculum to overt and covert forms of sexual harassment. We were drawn to their work because, like our work on the effect of racism on black and white people, the Sadker and Sadker (1994) focused on the effects of sexism on boys as well as on girls. The seminar took place in the early 1970s and served to broaden our views of systemic oppression in our schools. While our desegregation-related jobs were focused on issues of race, the issue of gender discrimination was similarly ubiquitous.

Initially, we found that we resisted conflating issues of race with issues of gender. Our concern was rooted in our belief that to address issues of sexism would cause those in power in our schools to address issues of gender at the expense of issues of race. We had engaged in a process that our friend and colleague, Glen Singleton (Singleton & Linton, 2006), two decades later would refer to as "Oppression Olympics." We had allowed ourselves to be entrapped into pitting issues of race against issues of gender in order to address racism. Once we made visible our *undiscussable,* namely fear of losing control, we saw that we could not choose among issues of oppression. All forms of oppression must be addressed. For us, this journey represented movement from cultural blindness to cultural precompetence.

In the early 1970s, sexism was made visible in all parts of the education community. Discriminatory practices in higher education, teacher assignments, and curriculum and instruction were arguably most prominent. University preparation programs were treating gender issues as if they were invisible. Women teachers predominated in elementary schools and, while there were women teaching in high schools, they were practically invisible in mathematics and science departments. Similarly, school administrators were overwhelmingly male (and white), so much so that it was rare to find women high school principals or superintendents. Curriculum and instruction were delivered in a manner to channel women high school students into "women's careers" such as elementary school teaching, nursing, and social work. Methodological studies (Sadker & Sadker, 1994) demonstrated that teachers' patterns of attention favored boys over girls. And, predictably, the invisibility of females from U.S. history contributed to distorted views of reality for both boys and girls.

The passage of Title IX, Education Amendments of 1972, and the Women's Education Equity Act in 1974 gave promise that our congressional leadership had the commitment of moral courage in addressing systemic gender inequities in our schools. However, in many ways, the struggle was just beginning with the passage of these acts due to the backlash from political groups who tied the struggle for gender equity to their own negative reaction to the rise of the modern feminist movement (Sadker & Sadker, 1994).

Gender issues may have experienced more progress in the last generation than have other cultural issues discussed in this book. Progress within secondary schools and university athletic programs is evident; and, many school districts are more attentive to addressing gender disparities in representation of male and female students into heretofore gender identified academic majors. In no way should progress be construed that parity or success has been attained, because certainly it has not. Recently, the Association for Supervision and Curriculum Development (2007) summarized key areas of Title IX that face ongoing challenges as follows:

- access to higher education in fields such as mathematics and science, which are closely tied to the future of job growth and professional school enrollment

- inequitable resources favoring male college athletes
- women still being overrepresented in traditional feminine-identified career fields (e.g., child care) with median salaries much lower than traditional male-identified careers (e.g., electricians)
- separate programs for pregnant and parenting students of comparable quality to other school programs
- complaints of sexual harassment in elementary and secondary schools
- standardized test gender achievement gap between African American, Latina, and Native American females when compared with white and Asian female students

Reflection

How would male and female students in your school describe how they are treated in your school? If your school has extra-curricular programs, what is the pattern of male and female student representation in the programs? Among the educators in your school, how are the voices of male and female faculty valued? Please record your responses in the space below.

_____

_____

_____

_____

Social Class Issues

It has been our experience that many educators prefer to use poverty or socioeconomic differences as an explanation for underachievement rather than attribute it to any of the other demographic issues discussed in this book. We are pleased that most state-level accountability and NCLB systems require student achievement data to be disaggregated by socioeconomic status in addition to race, language, and gender. Considering socioeconomic issues separate from other demographic groupings provides us with the opportunity to accurately assess needs and develop programs accordingly. Student and parental/guardian socioeconomic status must be a visible topic and not be allowed to persist as another of the "undiscussables" in our schools.

Education often is touted as the vehicle for social mobility in the United States and Canada. At the beginning of the twentieth century, few of what we now call school-age populations were attending school beyond sixth grade (Richardson, 1980; Unger, 2001). Since World War II, an increasing proportion of students from lower socioeconomic groups have been graduating from high school. Alongside this increase, federal and state programs have been implemented to address issues related to children from low-income communities.

It is important to recognize that mandatory universal education through grade twelve in the United States is a very modern occurrence. As a profession and as a country we are still in the "learning curve" of how best to educate students from low-income backgrounds, which is not dissimilar to our learning curve in responding to the educational needs of the other cultural groups described in this book. As of 2002, twenty-seven states had compulsory education requirements only to the attainment of age sixteen (Digest of Educational Statistics, 2005). For people from lower socioeconomic groups in the United States, the correlation with ethnicity and race is consistent. While the majority of people below the "poverty line" in the United States are white, the disproportionate numbers are people of color—African American, Latino, and First Nations People.

Three programs with long-standing histories in our schools serve the needs of students from low-income backgrounds—the free and reduced lunch program initiated in 1946, 1965's Elementary and Secondary Education Title I (i.e., the current manifestation is No Child Left Behind) and Head Start Programs. Added to these programs is the recent emphasis within state and federal mandates (e.g., NCLB) to disaggregate data using socioeconomic status as one of the student data groupings.

Reflection

Does your school or school district have any of the programs described above? How are Head Start and Title I students regarded in your school/district? When you hear colleagues at your school or from other schools talk about "Head Start" or "Title I" students, how do you understand their intent? How are the parents and guardians of these students regarded? When discussion of standards or assessment focuses on low socioeconomic students, how do you or your colleagues respond? Please enter your comments in the space provided.

_____

_____

_____

_____

Achievement Gaps Point to Leadership Vacuums

In Chapter 4, we discussed the constructive influence of No Child Left Behind (2002) in mandating that the schools address disparities in student achievement. Lindsey et al. (2008) held that the disparities are not only in "outcomes" as measured by the National Assessment of Educational Progress (Perie et al., 2005) but also in the "inputs" of who has access to high quality instruction and curriculum. Leadership is the extent to which educators can take the ethical and moral stance to address these issues within their schools. The good news is that educators now have "permission" to address disparities based on language, gender, and socioeconomic status within the provision of NCLB and many state-level reforms.

It is more than coincidence that achievement disparities correlate with students arriving at our schools fluent in a language other than English, or being female, or being from a low socioeconomic family. The struggle to provide equitable access has been underway for two generations. No Child Left Behind as well as numerous similar state measures now require that we provide the moral leadership in our schools to close the persistent gaps in access and achievement.

The tools of cultural proficiency provide a framework for individual educators and school communities to address disparities in access and achievement. Educators engaged in the journey to cultural proficiency learn of the impact their expectations have on all students. Furthermore, they learn how the organizational culture of the school facilitates the learning of, in the case of this chapter, English-speaking students, male students, and middle and upper socioeconomic students. The culturally proficient educator expands his repertoire of individual values and behaviors and his school's policies and practices to be inclusive of students' cultures in ways that facilitate learning.

THE CULTURAL PROFICIENCY CONTINUUM: A GUIDE FOR YOUR REFLECTIONS

The cultural proficiency continuum, introduced in Chapter 2, is reproduced as Table 5.1 for your convenience. The continuum is one of the tools of cultural proficiency and it provides language to describe unhealthy and healthy *values and behaviors* of persons and *policies and practices* of organizations. As you construct your responses to the prompts later in this chapter, you may find the continuum and the essential elements of cultural competence provide support in understanding your values and behaviors and your school's policies and practices. Please remember, movement along the continuum represents a shift in thinking from holding the view of *tolerating diversity* to *transformation for equity.*

As you read vignettes from our cultural autobiographies and construct your own recollections and reflections, please use the continuum as

Table 5.1   The Cultural Proficiency Continuum: A Guide for Your Reflections

Cultural Destructiveness		Cultural Blindness		Cultural Competence	
	Cultural Incapacity		Cultural Precompetence		Cultural Proficiency

a frequent reference point to gauge your and your school's resistance, regression, learning, and progress that make each of us effective in our diverse society.

To refresh your memory of the definitions for the points of the continuum, please refer to material in Chapter 2.

RANDY'S VIGNETTES—ONE PERSON'S EXPERIENCES

I became aware of social status early in life. We lived on the "other side" of the tracks in a neighborhood with few modern conveniences. However, in school I was accorded high-quality instruction and earned good grades to mark my academic progress. I selected the vignettes for this chapter that illustrate growing awareness of gender, language learners, and social class beginning in my family and progressing through my college days, teaching high school in California, and working with a desegregation team at Cal State, Los Angeles. Please read the vignettes for the purpose of understanding how these cultural experiences helped form my identity.

Gender roles in our extended family from Kentucky and Tennessee and the presence of religion were very similar to my experience in our hometown in Illinois. Men did men things and women did women things.

• •

Now that I am thinking about it, as a sophomore (1961) at WIU, in my introductory sociology class, Dr. Jane Stull had us find our social class on a nine-level schema. Each of the three social classes was further subdivided into three groups. After searching for my parents' level of education and employment, I was stunned to learn that I was in middle-lower class. I can still recall the mild shock and looking around at my classmates in embarrassment, hoping they didn't see my results. Though I had the distasteful experiences in my sixth grade class, it was this experience that made it a reality—I was lower class.

• •

(Continued)

(Continued)

This dynamic of who was assimilated in the school-tracking scheme became an education in privilege and entitlement. Unlike the subtlety practiced in Kankakee, the Hanford educators held tracking to a high value. The school had four tracks. From bottom to top they were—Z, Y, X and Advanced Placement. The lowest track, Z, was highly populated with Mexican Americans whereas they were almost invisible in the Advanced Placement sections. My first year as a teacher at the school, as an unknown, I was assigned to two sections of Z, two sections of Y, and one of X. In the spring I was informed that since I had proven myself in the first year that I would not have the Z track the next year.

One of my new colleagues, Kikanza, and Ray continued to push me to deal with my sexism and homophobia. It was a painful process and I wanted to stay tied to what I knew most and best—racism. Kikanza and Ray would have none of it. They challenged me by asking what made me think that as an adherent to equity that I had the right to pick and choose my —isms.

As a white male maturing in the 1950s to 1970s, my gender, social class, and ethnic identities were not materially affected. Through high school, college, and early in my career, I was able to choose whether or not to confront my own assumptions about those different from me and to benefit from inherent privileges that I could not see. There were few impediments to my social mobility. Ray's experience, as you will read, is similar yet different on issues of gender, language, and social class.

RAY'S VIGNETTES—ANOTHER PERSON'S EXPERIENCES

Like Randy, I became aware of issues of social class and gender early in my life. Due to my parents' jobs, we were working-class people who had a comfortable lifestyle. Gender roles were equitable, which was common for African American families where both parents worked in order for their children to have more than they had when they were young. As you will see, it was my time in the U.S. Navy where I became fully aware of social class across racial boundaries.

My mother worked as a domestic for one of the community's leading white families and my father was a laborer at a steel mill in a neighboring community. My parents' relationship was stable. Because both parents worked, it was my perception that we were fairly well off, a black family not experiencing any of the usual indicators of poverty . . . disconnected utilities, a lack of food, and we had one of the first televisions in our neighborhood. My mom had a fifth grade education and I discovered that she had difficulty reading when I brought her a note from high school and she had me read it to her. My dad had a sixth grade education but he was an avid reader and followed current events in the newspaper and by listening to daily newscasts.

* *

My father taught me to have great respect for women by example. As much as my mother and sisters doted on me, he actively pampered my mom and his three daughters. He did have a "boys will be boys" attitude that allowed me to get away with a wide range of mischievous acts if he discovered them. My mom, on the other hand, seemed to find no humor in my many escapades, and she became the chief disciplinarian. I later found out that she was often amused by many of my antics, but she was afraid that the larger community, particularly the larger white community, would not see the humor and that punishment from those forces could prove to be lethal.

* *

Two weeks after being discharged from the Navy I used the G. I. Bill and enrolled at Miami University in Oxford, Ohio, with hopes of pursuing psychology as my major. I was twenty-one-years-old with three and a half years of naval service. My classmates were eighteen-years-old, overwhelmingly white, and socioeconomically mostly upper middle-upper class. I stayed for a semester and a half at the university before dropping out. There were two major factors that influenced my decision. The first was the feeling of racial and socioeconomic isolation. I spent most of the time when I was in the Navy in racial isolation because of my workstation. However, most of the whites in that environment were at the same or even a lower socioeconomic background than mine. The university provided me my first experience with persons near my age who openly expressed and acted from positions of white, male, rich entitlement.

It was not until I became an educator that I became aware of the extensive limitations placed on people due to their native language, gender, or social class. My experiences at home, in the navy, and in college provided me the opportunity to develop an equity perspective that began with my own racial identity. I will always be grateful to my parents for the solid beginning they provided me.

YOUR PERSONAL EXPERIENCES WITH LANGUAGE, GENDER, AND SOCIAL CLASS

The preceding brief historical overview of past and present practices and vignettes from our experiences provides a context for understanding current disparities that exist in our society and schools. In this section, you will build on the information you compiled in Chapter 4 by recording your cross-cultural learning related to those whose primary language, gender, and social class are different from yours.

Table 5.2 provides you an opportunity to reflect on a personal experience in your life that contributed to your knowledge and skills of working with people whose primary language, gender, and social class are different from yours. It may be that the personal experience you choose to reflect on and describe is positive or negative for you and for the other person/people involved. The purpose of this activity is for you to construct a profile of the events in your life that have contributed to the development of your attitudes, values, and behaviors regarding issues of language acquisition, gender, and social class. This journey of understanding your own personal development will equip you to understand how the development and implementation of school policies and practices are also shaped in large part by our past experiences.

Now that you have had the opportunity to reflect on a past experience with someone whose primary language, gender, or social class is different from yours, again we challenge you to extend your personal learning journey by conducting a cultural interview.

Your Cultural Interview

You will recall that we use the term *challenge* with thoughtful intentionality. This book is designed as a personal journey *inward*—it is about *you* learning about *you* as a person, as an educator, and as a leader in cross-cultural situations. The cultural interview protocol set forth in Table 5.3 on page 78 provides the opportunity to learn about someone from a primary language, gender, or social class group different from yours. Table 5.4 on page 79 is for you to summarize your interview and to begin to analyze for themes and trends that emerge from the interview.

Please remember the two caveats for conducting the cultural interview. First, the value of the interview is to learn about the person being interviewed *and* to learn about your reactions to the material learned. Second, your interview with this person should not be construed as applying to all other people of their same cultural group. As you may recall from the description of the guiding principles of cultural proficiency in Chapter 2, there is as much diversity within cultures as there is among cultures. So, proceed with the knowledge that this is another step in your personal journey of cross-cultural learning.

Table 5.2   My Personal Experience

Language, Gender, and Social Class
My personal growth experiences with people from language, gender, or social class groups different from me. Briefly, these are my three experiences: • Our primary languages were different - • I am male and she was female; or, I am female and he was male - • The person was from a social class different from me -
What I did or my responses to the experiences: • The primary language experience - • The gender experience - • The social class experience -
What might I do the next time I encounter people different from me: • The primary language experience - • The gender experience - • The social class experience -
My lessons learned are . . .

Table 5.3   Cultural Interview

Language, Gender, and Social Class

1. How do you define yourself in terms of language, gender, or socioeconomic class?

2. How do you describe the structure of your family as you were growing up?

3. What is the primary language spoken in your home?

4. How do you *describe* the primary language spoken in your home?

5. How might you describe your views regarding the importance or purpose of education?

6. How might you describe customs you follow that are not reinforced in our schools?

7. How might you describe the importance of faith, religion, or spirituality in your family?

8. How might you describe your views of racial, ethnic, or national origin to people different from you?

9. How might you describe people of a sexual orientation different from you?

10. How might you describe gender roles in your family?

11. How might you describe your worldview (e.g., purpose of life)?

12. What is there about you and members of your cultural group you believe to be important but were not asked by me?

Table 5.4   Cultural Interview Summary Sheet

Language, Gender, and Social Class
Now that you have interviewed a person from a language, gender, or social class group different from yours, describe how this person is different and similar from you in terms of their:
Values
Beliefs
Customs
Traditions
Language
Worldview
What assumptions about people who are? from a language, gender, or social class group different from yours were challenged as a result of this interview?

Return to Your Cultural Autobiography

In this chapter, you have read about issues that arise from language, gender, and social class differences. Once again, you have had the opportunity to reflect on past experiences, to interview people different from you, and to synthesize that information. We invite you to return to the cultural autobiography you began in Chapter 3 and to add and modify it accordingly, given the new information. Please remember that your cultural autobiography becomes increasingly useful as you probe ever more deeply into and learn from your experiences.

Where Are You on the Continuum?

Take a few minutes and review your Personal Experience and Interview notes from this language acquisition, gender, and social class. What feelings are being generated at this point in your "inside-out" journey? How might your reactions be similar or different to your responses at the end of Chapter 4?

_____

_____

_____

_____

For Further Reading

The following books are recommended both for your personal reading and for use with book studies with your colleagues. The recommended books are representative of the many fine works available for professional development:

Gilligan, Carol. (1983). *In a different voice.* Cambridge, MA: Harvard University Press.

Sadker, Myra, & Sadker, David. (1994). *Failing at fairness: How America's schools cheat girls.* New York: Charles Scribner's Sons.

Sleeter, Christine E., & Grant, Carl A. (2007). *Making choices for multicultural education: Five approaches to race, class, and gender* (2nd ed.). New York: Macmillan.

Zinn, Howard. (2003). *A people's history of the United States: 1492 to present.* New York: Harper Collins.

Responding to Issues Related to Sexual Orientation, Faith, and Ableness

6

. . . we do not know each other, and we may look strange (even ominous) in each other's eyes, but we occupy the same territory, belong to the same human community, and we need to acknowledge that fact and learn to get along.

—Parker Palmer (1997, p. 39)

GETTING CENTERED

Few issues in our schools are more present and simultaneously treated as invisible and undiscussable than issues of sexual orientation, faith, and ableness. It seems that in our schools we often try to render these issues invisible; yet, each is present whether affirmed or not. In the same manner that began the introductions to Chapters 4 and 5, think of times when you have overheard or been part of conversations that involved issues of sexual orientation, faith, or ableness. What did you hear? What did you feel then and now? How did you react or respond at the time? How do you wish you had responded?

_____

_____

_____

_____

Sexual orientation is a topic most often avoided and one that can elicit reactions and responses based on people's expressed religious values. Similarly, issues of faith, long professed to be separate from the domains of schooling, are expressed through the values most educators bring to school. Issues of faith give rise to questions such as whose values are to be central in the school and to the religion versus secularism debates that occur throughout the country and are most visible during election years. If the topics of Chapters 4 and 5 provoke difficult conversations, issues related to sexual orientation, faith, and ableness raise the threshold for skillful facilitation of difficult conversations for many of us. While colleagues and students may be of a faith or sexual orientation different from us, these issues are rarely on our professional development agendas.

In contrast, students with special needs, who are visible in our schools and part of our professional development agenda, too often are viewed as being the responsibility of special educators. The current accountability movement spawned by NCLB and state-level school reforms has made the education of students with special needs visible to all educators.

Providing equitable educational opportunities for students based on their sexual orientation, faith, and ableness is a growing topic in our schools. The intent of this chapter, as with the previous chapters, is to provide you with a moral centeredness when confronting the *undiscussables* within your own journey and by making them normal and every day topics of discussion in our schools. The too often *undiscussables* in this chapter are related to the sexual orientation, faith, and ableness of our students.

HISTORICAL CONTEXT: SEXUAL ORIENTATION, FAITH, AND ABLENESS

The positioning of these topics together into one chapter may seem uniquely coincidental to you the reader. As indicated in the Introduction to this book, we have organized this book in approximately the sequence the topics emerged into our, the authors', consciousness and provoked actions on our part. Though ableness, as expressed through special education programs, has been present throughout our careers, it was later in our careers that it emerged as an issue of access and inclusion for us in the same way we regard race and ethnicity. Making issues of sexual orientation, faith, and ableness visible in our work is an example of our, the authors', own cultural blindness and our own continuous journey toward cultural proficiency.

Issues of sexual orientation and faith emerged somewhat simultaneously for us. Though each of us was raised in culturally religious environments, and had opportunities to interact with religions different from ours, it is the emergence of issues of sexual orientation and the counter-vailing pressures from some religious groups that has pushed both issues into our consciousness.

The information presented in this chapter is drawn from sources in addition to our own personal and professional experiences. You may want to consult some of the many excellent books that present detailed descriptions and cogent rationales for inclusive education with regard to sexual orientation (Bochenek & Brown, 2001; Miller, 2006), faith (Townley & Schmeider-Ramirez, 2007) and, ableness (Baca & Almanza, 1991; Gollnick & Chinn, 2006). These works can serve as resources for your own continued personal and professional development and your school's book studies.

Sexual Orientation

The issue rendered most undiscussable in our schools is sexual orientation. Reports of bullying, sexual harassment, and discrimination based on sexual orientation are beginning to emerge. Students' education is compromised when lesbian, gay, bisexual, transgendered, and intersex students and faculty are objects of physical and psychological intimidation and abuse. The resulting feelings of powerlessness by those affected limit their ability to participate fully in their own education and careers (Bochenek & Brown, 2001).

Discounting of students due to their sexual orientation exists when students can't see themselves in the curriculum or when other students don't see positive and accurate portrayal of lesbian, gay, bisexual, transgendered, or intersex (LGBTI) members of our society. When LGBTI students don't see accurate portrayals of themselves in the curriculum, they experience an invisibility that mirrors their daily existence. Similarly, when heterosexual students are denied an authentic representation of lesbian, gay, bisexual, transgendered, and intersex members in our history and present society, they have a skewed vision of their own prominence reminiscent of the whitewashed curriculum of the pre-Civil Rights era.

In North America, widely different protections are afforded people based on their sexual orientation. In the province of Ontario, the home to one third of Canadians, protection from discrimination and harassment based on sexual orientation is derived from the United Nations' Universal Declaration of Human Rights which claims that *recognition of the inherent dignity and the equal and inalienable rights of all members of the human family is the foundation of freedom, justice and peace in the world* (Human Rights, Code 1990). In contrast within the U.S., as of 2002, only the states of California, Connecticut, Vermont, and Wisconsin explicitly prohibit discrimination based on sexual orientation (Bochenek & Brown, 2001).

In the United States, recurring efforts to expand the language of the due process clause of the Fourteenth Amendment to include protections for sexual orientation are met with stringent counterarguments within Congress and in our federal courts. California's recently signed Senate Bill 777, which is designed to protect lesbian, gay, transgendered, and bisexual students from discrimination, is facing fierce resistance from conservative forces trying to cast it as another example of the "gay agenda to undermine the traditional family."

The physical bullying and discrimination of LGBTI students and faculty are topics that stay under the radar with members of the dominant group complicit in the resulting repression of these members. It is an issue that will not subside and rests, in large part, on the courage of school leaders to step forward and address the underlying moral issue of basic human rights. We can't conceive of a democratic society condoning quasi-religious bigotry being allowed to drive social policy much longer. Our country's experience when slavery, racism, and sexism were advocated from some church pulpits was finally overcome. The time is here for human rights to be inalienable.

Reflection

When you think about sexual orientations different from yours, what images emerge for you? When colleagues at your school or school district discuss educational issues that face lesbian, gay, bisexual, transgendered, or intersex students and faculty, how would you characterize the discussions? How do you react to this information in this section? Please enter your responses in the space provided.

_____

_____

_____

_____

Issues of Faith

Any student of United States and Canadian histories can't escape the role that religion played in the European migrations to North America. At the same time, most of our history books rarely honor the faith or spiritual practices of the indigenous populations or the populations forcibly brought to this continent, most notably from Africa as slaves. Our histories of migration and conquest are too often mixed in with stories of Europeans escaping to North America due to religious persecution in their homelands and initially settling in isolated enclaves. While the experiences of conquest and exploitation of Africans, First Nations People, and Europeans fleeing persecutions in their homelands are all factual, it is only the Europeans' story that comprises the dominant narrative in our national curriculum.

In the isolated enclaves that became the U.S. colonies, the struggle over religious perspectives and practices, along with the abiding concern over state-sponsored religions, led Thomas Jefferson and James Madison to insure that the U.S. Constitution provide for a separation of church and state. The "establishment clause" in the First Amendment of the U.S. Constitution holds that *Congress shall make no law respecting the establishment of religion, or prohibiting the free exercise thereof* (Townley & Schmeider-Ramirez, 2007). The effect is that each person is guaranteed religious freedom and is free from state-sponsored religion.

However, given that our schools are microcosms of the larger society, forces continue to militate that raise faith-based issues for educators to address. Over forty years ago, required school prayers were declared unconstitutional and since that time school prayers at graduations and other public school events continue to be debated in the court of public opinion. The U.S. Supreme Court issued a test of three questions to determine a standard for whether or not school actions violated the establishment clause of the First Amendment to the U.S. Constitution:

- Does the action have a secular purpose?
- Does the action have an effect that neither advances nor impedes religion?
- Does the action avoid excessive entanglement with religion? (Townley & Schmeider-Ramirez, 2007).

In setting this standard, the court held that if any action failed any one of these questions, it was unconstitutional. In whatever way this decision helped clarify the parameters for school-sponsored religious activities, it did not make them go away. Today, numerous faith-based issues are front and center in many school communities:

- Issues of teaching evolution versus teaching creationism are actively debated in some state legislatures and departments of education.
- Issues over the presence of Christmas trees, or viewing Halloween as a pagan experience, or the presence of religious icons in schools continue to be active topics in some of our communities.
- Issues as to whether it is an expression of free speech to wear clothing with language that declares homosexuality as sinful has been and is being tested in state and federal courts.

- Emerging issues are the manner in which our schools respect and protect the rights of some groups to wear their religious dress in schools.

Once again, the intent of this brief review is to illustrate the presence of the topic within our schools. It is not our intent to present an exhaustive review of the pros and cons of the issue but to provoke your thinking about where you are with the presence or absence of faith in your professional life and your cognizance of how you respond to those who have views and practices different from yours.

Reflection

How do you describe the dominant religious or faith perspective in your school? How might faculty or parents who are not represented by the dominant perspective describe it?

How would students from smaller faith communities in your school describe how they are treated in your school? Among the educators in your school, how do you recognize colleagues' perspectives that are based within their faiths? How would you describe your own faith-based perspective? Is it okay in your school to not have a faith or spiritual orientation? How do you know? Please record your responses in the space below.

_____

_____

_____

_____

Ableness

One of the common denominators experienced by each of the demographic groups that are the focus of this book is that their rights have had to be amended into the social contract of our country and our schools. In other words, the inclusion of students regardless of their ableness is due to legislative and judicial actions sought by those who had been excluded or marginalized from our schools. Prior to 1970, only 20 percent of students with special needs were in schools. For all practical purposes they were rendered invisible to the larger society who did not have them as members of their own families or other close-knit communities.

Proponents of providing for the educational needs of students with special needs used the due process clause of the *1954 Brown v. Topeka* U.S. Supreme Court decision to gain access to our public schools. Since 1975, landmark legislation has been crafted and implemented to provide equitable educational opportunities to special needs populations. Principle among federal laws are Public Law 94–142, Education for All Handicapped Children Act (1975); Public Law 101–476, Individuals with Disabilities Act (1990); and H.R. 1350, Reauthorization of IDEA (2004) (as cited in Townley, & Schmeider-Ramirez, 2007), which is designed to apply the standards-reforms of NCLB to students with special needs.

Questions about how best to educate students with special needs continue an ongoing discussion first begun in the early 1970s. Issues of funding, mainstreaming, development and implementation of students' Individual Education Plans, student discipline, and meeting NCLB required academic assessments are front and center in most school districts.

In many of our schools and university preparation programs, special education programs and regular education programs are treated as separate and distinct programs. However, the issue of students with special needs having to meet the rigorous standards set forth by NCLB has raised new levels of concerns among educators. Now that special education students are one of the demographic groups tested in meeting NCLB standards (Latham, Latham, & Mandlawitz, 2008), many school leaders acknowledge the scores of students with special needs in annual statewide assessments keep the school from being in full compliance with NCLB. Coupled with widespread negative reaction to NCLB being regarded by many educator groups as an unfunded mandate, the education of students with special needs continues to be a provocative subject in many schools and school districts.

Who is to be taught in our schools and to what levels of academic mastery is the equity topic of the twenty-first century. A hundred years ago it would have been inconceivable to entertain the idea of educating the demographic groups of students addressed in this book, let alone students with special needs. The manner in which our democracy continues to unfold and include groups historically excluded, either advertently or inadvertently, is linked to the manner to which society ceases to limit access to educational opportunities. The role of schools, in particular public schools, is an important component in leading a democracy characterized by diversity, access, and inclusion.

Reflection

Does your school have students with special needs? If so, how are these students regarded by faculty and other students? In what manner do special educators and regular educators communicate in your school? When you hear colleagues in your school discuss the students with special needs, what are they saying? How are these students and their parents regarded? When discussion of standards or assessment focuses on students with special needs, how do you or your colleagues respond? Please enter your comments in the space provided.

_____

_____

_____

_____

Moral Leadership Is Tested in New Ways

Of the three topics discussed in this chapter, only one—ableness—is addressed in current school reform initiatives. School leaders who view their role as advocating for the invisible or voiceless will be sensitive to and aware of the experiences of LGBTI students, students from nondominant faiths, and students who do not subscribe to religious practices.

As we discussed in Chapters 4 and 5, addressing issues of academic and access achievement gaps is a moral issue. How we approach and deal with the treatment of students based on their sexual orientation, faith, and ableness is a test of educational leaders' commitment to an inclusive democratic society. By now, you recognize that the tools of cultural proficiency are designed for educators intent on providing all students a high quality education.

THE CULTURAL PROFICIENCY CONTINUUM: A GUIDE FOR YOUR REFLECTIONS

The cultural proficiency continuum introduced in Chapter 2 is reproduced as Table 6.1 for your convenience. As you will recall, it provides language to describe unhealthy and healthy *values and behaviors* of persons and *policies and practices* of organizations. As you construct your responses to the prompts later in this chapter, you may find the continuum and the essential elements of cultural competence provide support in understanding your values and behaviors and your school's policies and practices. Please remember, movement along the continuum represents a shift in thinking from holding the view of *tolerating diversity* to *transformation for equity*.

As you read vignettes from our cultural autobiographies and construct your own recollections and reflections, please use the continuum as a frequent reference point to gauge your and your school's resistance, regression, learning, and progress that each of us make to be effective in our diverse society.

Table 6.1   The Cultural Proficiency Continuum: A Guide for Your Reflections

Cultural Destructiveness		Cultural Blindness		Cultural Competence	
	Cultural Incapacity		Cultural Precompetence		Cultural Proficiency

To refresh your memory of the definitions for the points of the continuum, please refer to material in Chapter 2 or 4. It is evident that a person can be at multiple points on the continuum depending on the cultural groups being considered. When we decided to write this book based on our personal and professional experiences, it was with the conviction that we be inclusive. Educating all students is our mission and being mindful of cultural issues that impede and facilitate our success is important. Though issues related to sexual orientation, faith, and ableness are not new in our schools, they may be new in your professional conversations.

RAY'S VIGNETTES—ONE PERSON'S EXPERIENCES

My experience with issues related to religion, sexual orientation, and ableness emerged at different times in my life. In the following vignettes you will read of the influence of religion in my home, my first knowledge of sexual orientation, and developing an understanding of ableness.

*My parents were very religious. My dad was a deacon in the local Baptist church and my mom sang in the choir. I joined the church when I was about ten years old. I also sang in the choir and served on the usher board. As I grew older, I developed my own philosophy of religion. I consider myself a very spiritual being, but I am skeptical of organized religions. I know that church and the interactions around them serve an essential purpose in the lives of many people. I also know that deep-rooted beliefs can also be a source of division between and among people. I often wonder if it's possible to be a true believer of any form of religion and at the same time **value** those who hold totally different beliefs.*

(Continued)

(Continued)

The military was also a time when I first encountered a cultural reality that had never been discussed in my small hometown. I had no knowledge or experience with anyone who was homosexual. The lack of knowledge also meant that I had no feelings of bias for different sexual orientations. One of my shipmates "hit" on me one day. I didn't at first realize what he was asking me. He explained the attraction that he felt for me and how he wished to express his affection. I was curious, and he was willing to engage in an ongoing discussion explaining his feelings, when he was aware of them, and how natural they were for him. He introduced me to other gay men that he knew and a lesbian couple who shared an apartment in Long Beach. I became an adopted member in the community. While there were other shipmates who then began to believe that I might be homosexual, I was always comfortable enough with myself to not be threatened.

* * *

There was an early experience with ableness that had a profound effect on me. We had a cousin named Sonny. Sonny was physically deformed with both his hands and feet being webbed, his head being pointed and his eyes being enlarged. He operated mentally at the level of an eight-year-old. Sonny was institutionalized in a state hospital, but he was allowed home visits. When he came to stay with us for two or three two-week visits a year, we shared a bedroom because I was the only boy in the house. The visits occurred for me between the ages of five–fifteen before Sonny died.

At first all of my friends were afraid of Sonny because of the way that he looked and talked, and they would make fun of him. I knew Sonny as a warm, gentle, caring person who loved baseball, especially the Cincinnati Reds. He knew statistics, batting averages, players, and histories. We listened to every game on the radio when he visited. He also liked to do little favors for anyone in the house. I finally had to confront some of my friends and ended one friendship because she refused to accept Sonny. This living experience provided me with insights into how persons could be cruel to someone who was physically and mentally disabled. It was clear to me that this was a form of discrimination based on appearances and a basic ignorance of the person that Sonny was. It was also clear to me that this was a form of bias and discrimination that I always committed to confronting and changing.

Reading my vignettes may have caused questions such as these to surface for you:

- As a person who has an affirmed religious orientation or who chooses a nonreligious or spiritual perspective, how do you respond to students or colleagues different from you?
- As a gay or straight person, in what manner are these issues part of the everyday conversations about your students and the community you serve?

- In what manner are differently abled students a part of your school and your daily reality?

These and similar questions may be part of your reflections or your interview. Randy's vignettes will prompt you to continue examining your own life and to look for the bases of your assumptions and values.

RANDY'S VIGNETTES—ANOTHER PERSON'S EXPERIENCES

In my formative years, religion was ever present, though church attendance was not. Issues related to sexual orientation and ableness were all but invisible. I do recall smutty comments about certain members of the local women's softball team but was not aware of sexual orientation until a college sociology class. Interestingly, the course title included the term "criminology." Ableness in my world was almost limited to wounded war veterans and a neighbor boy with cerebral palsy. I selected the following vignettes to portray the insular world in which I lived and to help me understand that I can choose how to deal with these issues, which supports an example of entitlement that continues to constrain many of our schools.

Religion was comprised of things to fear, but gospel songs were uplifting. Formal religious training was largely absent. For that reason, my parents joined the First United Methodist Church. They thought it was time for my sister and me to be baptized and confirmed. I have wonderful recollections of the pastor at the time, Dr. Loyal M. Thompson, but the church experience was seemingly social. I enjoyed the opportunity to be with other students my age and the history part of the Sunday school classes was usually interesting. I was aware that the kids in my school were of varying religions but it didn't seem to be an issue. However, adults could name the three Jewish families in town.

· ·

Religion didn't appear to me to be an issue in my high school. However, it did occur in my home when my mother learned I was dating a Catholic girl. It was a muted objection that didn't last long, however I remember being stunned by the very raising of the issue. Over the ensuing years I was to learn that cross-cultural issues were often tested at the "dating age." The other occurrence was when my grandmother referred to her physician as "that Jewish doctor." It was never expressed in malevolence, only as a matter of fact as if it was part of his name. Christian physicians were not similarly identified.

· ·

(Continued)

(Continued)

Almost as oblivious was my awareness of the special education class in our junior high school building. I knew nothing of the students because they had their own classroom, their own teacher, and were identified by the use of terms such as EMR and TMR. There was little or no contact between the students from that classroom and our students. Too often, the special education students were the objects of jokes from both the regular education students and we educators.

....

During that year (1972) I had my initial sexual orientation experience. All of the teachers new to the district were required to take my several session course, Developing New Perspective on Race. The course started well and all who were supposed to be in attendance did so each week until about the sixth week when one of the members quit coming. After a few missed sessions, I called him to inquire about his absences. He asked for a private meeting to discuss his concerns with the course. We met at a local bar where he proceeded to tell me how much he enjoyed the course but his big fear was that our climate of openness might make him feel too comfortable and to share with the group that he was gay. I was dumbfounded. Though I was well aware of issues of sexual orientation, I had never (knowingly) talked with a gay person. I was immediately aware of my feelings of uneasiness in his presence. The meeting ended amicably and he agreed to return to the course but would probably be reticent to be open. He conceded that if he revealed his sexual orientation that he would most likely be released from his contract. He was most likely correct.

I recall at the time being conflicted. Part of me was deeply bothered that people experienced the types of overt discrimination that my gay colleague described to me. I didn't want him to lose his job as I regarded him to be an excellent teacher. At the same time, I was fully aware of my feelings of avoidance. I had occasion to raise my colleague's dilemma with Ray and Nancy later and during the discussion to share my feelings of avoidance. Ray and Nancy pushed me very hard and asked me, "What gives you the right to decide which equity issues you agree to support and those you don't? Isn't that an ultimate form of entitlement?" That heated discussion rings in my ears thirty years later. I was beginning to see the benefit of having cultural informants as a means to be able to see my own assumptions.

To the extent that *undiscussables* are avoided in our schools, issues related to sexual orientation, faith, and ableness are routinely avoided. Making cultural issues visible is basic to examining how students are represented and valued in our schools. We trust you will use the following interview protocol to extend your own learning in a way that supports your being an effective educator.

YOUR PERSONAL EXPERIENCES WITH SEXUAL ORIENTATION, FAITH, AND ABLENESS

The preceding brief historical overview of past and present practices and vignettes from our experiences provide a context for understanding current disparities that exist in our society and schools. In this section, you are to build on the information you compiled in Chapters 4 and 5 by recording your cross-cultural learning related to those whose sexual orientation, faith, and ableness are different from yours.

Table 6.2 on page 94 provides you an opportunity to reflect on a personal experience in your life that contributed to your knowledge and skills of working with people whose sexual orientation, faith, and ableness are different from yours. It may be that the personal experience you choose to reflect on and describe is positive or negative for you and for the other person/people involved. The purpose of this activity is for you to construct a profile of the events in your life that have contributed to the development of your attitudes, values, and behaviors regarding issues of sexual orientation, faith, and ableness. This journey of understanding your own personal development will equip you to understand how the development and implementation of school policies and practices are also shaped in large part by our past experiences.

Now that you have had the opportunity to reflect on a past experience with a person whose sexual orientation, faith, or ableness is different from you, again we challenge you to extend your personal learning journey by conducting a cultural interview.

Your Cultural Interview

We continue to use the term *challenge* with thoughtful intentionality. This book is designed as a personal journey *inward*—it is about *you* learning about *you* as a person, as an educator, and as a leader in cross-cultural situations. The cultural interview protocol set forth in Table 6.3 on page 95 provides the opportunity to learn about someone from a sexual orientation, faith, or ableness group different from you. Table 6.4 on page 96 is for you to summarize your interview and to begin to analyze for themes and trends that emerge from the interview.

Please remember the two caveats for conducting the cultural interview. First, the value of the interview is to learn about the person being interviewed *and* to learn about your reactions to the material learned. Second, your interview with this person should not be construed as applying to all other people of their same cultural group.

Table 6.2   My Personal Experience

Sexual Orientation, Faith, and Ableness

My personal growth experience with someone who is from a sexual orientation, faith, or ableness group different from me. Briefly, these are my three experiences:

- We were of different sexual orientation -

- We were from different faiths -

- We were from different ableness groups -

What I did or my response to the experiences:

- The sexual orientation experience -

- The faith experience -

- The ableness experience -

What might I do the next time I encounter people different from me:

- The sexual orientation experience -

- The faith experience -

- The ableness experience -

- My lessons learned are . . .

Table 6.3   Cultural Interview

Sexual Orientation, Faith, and Ableness

1. How do you define yourself in terms of sexual orientation, faith, or ableness?

2. How do you describe the structure of your family as you were growing up?

3. What is the primary language spoken in your home?

4. How do you *describe* the primary language spoken in your home?

5. How might you describe your views regarding the importance or purpose of education?

6. How might you describe customs you follow that are not reinforced in our schools?

7. How might you describe the importance of faith, religion, or spirituality in your family?

8. How might you describe your views of sexual orientation, faith, or ableness to people different from you?

9. How might you describe people of a sexual orientation different from you?

10. How might you describe people who have mental and physical abilities different from you?

11. How might you describe gender roles in your family?

12. How might you describe your worldview (e.g., purpose of life)?

13. What is there about you and members of your cultural group you believe to be important but were not asked by me?

Table 6.4   Cultural Interview Summary Sheet

Sexual Orientation, Faith, and Ableness
Now that you have interviewed a person from a sexual orientation, faith, or ableness group different from yours, describe how this person is different from and similar to you in terms of their:
Values
Beliefs
Customs
Traditions
Language
Worldview
What assumptions about people who are from a sexual orientation, faith, or ableness group different from yours were challenged as a result of this interview?

As you may recall from the description of the guiding principles of cultural proficiency in Chapter 2, there is as much diversity within cultures as there is among cultures. Please proceed with the knowledge that this is another step in your personal journey of cross-cultural learning.

Return to Your Cultural Autobiography

This chapter had you read about issues that arise from differences in sexual orientation, faith, and ableness. Your reflections on past experiences, your interviews with people different from you, and your synthesis of that information all add to your awareness of the cultural groups around you and about how you respond to them. Please take the opportunity to return to the cultural autobiography you began in Chapter 3 and add to and modify it accordingly given the additional new information. You may notice that your autobiography is beginning to expand who you are into being the person you want to become.

Where Are You on the Continuum?

Take a few minutes and review your Personal Experience and Interview notes from this sexual orientation, faith, and ableness. What feelings are being generated at this point in your "inside-out" journey? How might your reactions be similar or different to your responses at the end of Chapters 4 and 5?

_____

_____

_____

_____

For Further Reading

The following books are recommended both for your personal reading and for use with book studies with your colleagues. The recommended books are representative of the many fine works available for professional development:

Armstrong, Karen. (1993). *A history of God: The 4000-year quest of Judaism, Christianity and Islam.* New York: Random House.

Bochenek, Michael, & Brown, A. Widney. (2001). *Hatred in the hallways: Violence and discrimination against lesbian, gay, bisexual and transgender students in U.S. schools.* New York: Human Rights Watch.

Kozol, Jonathan. (2007). *Letters to a young teacher.* New York: Crown Publishers.

Miller, Neil. (2006). *Out of the past: Gay and lesbian history from 1869 to the present.* New York: Alyson Books.

Palmer, Parker. (1997). *The company of strangers, Christians and the renewal of America's public life.* New York: The Crossroad Publishing Company.

Part III

Leading From an Ethical Framework

Culturally Competent and Proficient Leadership Actions

7

As school leaders, we are here today to learn with our presenter.

—Denise Seguine, Executive Director of Learning,
Wichita Public Schools (October 3, 2006)

GETTING CENTERED

Learning is at the center of what educators are about—we teach and we learn. We earn our degrees and state-conferred credentials in order to teach and to lead. Take a moment and remember a time in your college/university experience or in a professional development session when you had an "aha" moment. Then, think of a time when you witnessed a classmate or colleague having an "aha" moment. What do you recall about your or their nonverbal expressions, verbal comments, and perceived insights? Please write your responses in the space below.

_____

_____

_____

_____

Learning can be a solitary or social activity. Culturally competent and proficient actions involve personal learning that may challenge long-held assumptions and values and cause you to behave in new ways. As a social construct, cultural competence and proficiency facilitates you and your colleagues' learning in community, and helps align your behaviors and your school's practices and policies to embrace the new learning. Sensing your personal "connections" and seeing them occur for your colleagues is rewarding.

Ms. Seguine's comment in the epigram above was part of her introduction of Randy to the administrators of the Wichita schools. We include her comment because it represents a frame of reference for professional development that is, unfortunately, not widespread in many of our schools. Too often we experience professional development as something administrators do "to" teachers rather than "with" teachers. We suspect this trend is even more prevalent when the topic is diversity related. In stark contrast, Ms. Seguine and her colleagues participate in mutual learning with their consultants. It was a true seminar in that all were learners. Randy's experience as a presenter was of engagement with a highly-involved group of colleagues in such a way that his learning was extended by the manner in which participants made connections to the cultural proficiency topics. It was also an example of how the role of educational leader is shared among members of the leadership team.

The role of educational leader in our nation's schools has evolved as the student population has become increasingly diverse. As our country continues to mature toward its promise of a true democracy, the PreK–12 schools are a linchpin to an inclusive society. Barely a hundred years ago, formal education was the province of a small portion of the populace. Since World War II, public education has expanded to include larger portions of the cultural groups discussed in this book. Your school, like all schools, is diverse in ways that were not recognized a generation ago. Formal and nonformal school leaders have great opportunity to insure that all cultural groups of our children and youth are well educated.

Your recorded experiences in Chapters 4–6 are designed to support you in your desire to be increasingly effective in cross-cultural settings. In this chapter, we now provide you with opportunities to continue your learning with us and to become intentionally competent and proficient.

Culturally competent and proficient professional development engages educators individually and collectively. As you reflect on your responses to the activities in Chapters 4–6, most likely you are aware of how rare it is to have these topics as part of the intentional, everyday conversations in our schools.

LINKING YOUR WORK TO THE
TOOLS OF CULTURAL PROFICIENCY

The assumptions we make with this book are that:

- You are a serious student of yourself, your students, your school, and the community your school serves.
- You do not have to be convinced of the efficacy of your students or your community to be educated.
- You believe that it is your responsibility to find ways to teach students in your school, and you believe cultural proficiency provides you the necessary lens to do your work as an educator.

For these reasons, we focus on the right-hand, transformational side of the continuum (see Table 2.2 on page 25) and have you focus on culturally precompetent, competent, and proficient values and behaviors to develop your leadership plan.

In this chapter we provide you with the means to summarize your reflections and interviews from Chapters 4, 5, and 6. You may want to refresh your knowledge of the tools by referring back to Chapter 2. The tools provide a context for intentional leadership development in these ways:

- The **guiding principles** show the way to build a powerful moral and philosophical framework for professional practice (see Table 2.1 on page 24). Simply stated, either you believe students can learn and be taught or you don't. Students' culture is used as an asset and dominant culture is recognized for its intent to limit access and opportunity.
- The **continuum** provides language for describing healthy and unhealthy values, behaviors, policies, and practices existing in our schools (see Table 2.2 on page 25). From the continuum you can determine whether you, or your school, focus on what is wrong with students or on what you can do differently to educate students.
- The **barriers** describe impediments to change as preserving the status quo (see Table 2.4 on page 27). Knowledge of the barriers helps you to see the extent to which the status quo serves selected groups of students and/or the educators.
- The **five essential elements** are the standards for educators' values and behaviors and schools' policies and practices (Table 2.3, which is included on the page that follows for ease of reference as Table 7.1). The essential elements exist at the cultural competence point of the continuum and are used to guide intentional leadership practice.

Take a few moments and read Table 7.1 (a repeat of Table 2.3). We have added leadership illustrations to the five essential elements. Pay

Table 7.1   The Essential Elements for Culturally Proficient Leadership

- **Assessing Cultural Knowledge**—Leading the learning about others' cultures, about how educators and the school as a whole react to others' cultures, and what you need to do to be effective in cross-cultural situations. Also, leading for learning about the school and its grade levels and departments as cultural entities.
- **Valuing Diversity**—Creating informal and formal decision-making groups inclusive of people whose viewpoints and experiences are different from yours and the dominant group at the school, and that will enrich conversations, decision making, and problem solving.
- **Managing the Dynamics of Difference**—Modeling problem solving and conflict resolution strategies as a natural and normal process within the organizational culture of the schools and the cultural contexts of the communities of your school.
- **Adapting to Diversity**—Being the lead learner at your school about cultural groups different from your own and the ability to use others' cultural experiences and backgrounds in all school settings.
- **Institutionalizing Cultural Knowledge**—Making learning about cultural groups and their experiences and perspectives an integral part of the school's professional development.

particular attention to the action words. The five essential elements of cultural proficiency are the standards used to frame your intentional leadership plan.

As an educator interested in the experiences of all cultural groups in your school, you continue to learn about your knowledge of and your response to groups different from yours. At the same time, you are a catalyst for ongoing learning among colleagues in your school. The five essential elements are professional standards you will use:

- to frame your journey within
- to craft an intentional plan for culturally proficient leadership

ANALYZING YOUR DATA TO BUILD A LEADERSHIP PLAN

In this section we have you return to your recorded responses in the Personal Growth Experiences and the Cultural Interviews in Chapters 4, 5, and 6. The following three-step process to synthesize information recorded in Chapters 4, 5, and 6 guides you in the initial stages of developing your leadership plan.

Step One: Your Placement on the Continuum

Review your responses to the final activity in Chapters 4, 5, and 6 and record below where you are on the continuum for each of the cultural groups:

- Race, ethnicity, national origin
- Language
- Gender
- Social Class
- Sexual Orientation
- Faith
- Ableness

For the cultural groups that you identified yourself as being at the destructiveness, incapacity, and blindness points of the continuum you will need to pause and determine the barriers in your life that impede you. The fact that you have persevered this far in the book is encouraging and the progress is two-phased:

1. Review the barriers to cultural proficiency (Table 2.4 on page 27) to determine what it is that blocks your progress toward precompetence and competence.

2. Ask yourself, "What is it about this cultural group that I need to know or that I fear? What additional knowledge or courage would I need to summon to face these self-imposed barriers?"

Please use the space below to record your responses.

_____

_____

_____

_____

For the cultural groups that you identified yourself as being at the pre-competent, competent, or proficiency points of the continuum, you are ready to move to Step Two and plan your leadership journey.

Step Two: Synthesizing Your Personal Growth Experiences

Examine your responses to the personal growth experiences in Tables 4.2 (on p. 59), 5.2 (on p. 77), and 6.2 (on p. 94). With particular focus on the "lessons learned" in each of the tables, take a few minutes and respond to these prompts:

- Describe the themes that emerge across your personal growth experiences (e.g., levels of comfort or discomfort; similarities or differences among the experiences).

  _____
  _____
  _____
  _____

- Describe insights you have to your values and assumptions prevalent in your cross-cultural relationships (e.g., derived from family members, friends, institutions).

  _____
  _____
  _____
  _____

- In thinking of the topics covered in this book, describe areas of future growth for yourself (e.g., knowledge of groups; how you might do things differently "the next time").

  _____
  _____
  _____
  _____

- Describe the leadership implications of your areas of future growth (e.g., particular cultural/demographic groups you want to learn more about; reaction of colleagues to particular cultural/ demographic groups).

  _____
  _____
  _____
  _____

Step Three: Synthesizing Your Interview Results

Next, examine and synthesize your responses to the section "assumptions about people who are different from you" from the Interview Summary Tables 4.4 (on p. 61), 5.4 (on p. 79), and 6.4 (on p. 96). As with the previous writing activity, take a few moments and record your responses in the spaces below:

- Describe the themes that emerge in your assumptions across this diverse set of interviews (e.g., levels of comfort or discomfort; similarities or differences among the experiences).

_____

_____

_____

_____

- Describe insights you have to these assumptions prevalent in your cross-cultural relationships and ways in which they are similar or different from the previous personal growth experience (e.g., derived from family members, friends, institutions).

_____

_____

_____

_____

- Describe areas of future growth revealed through your interviews (e.g., knowledge of groups; how you might do things differently "the next time").

_____

_____

_____

_____

- Describe the leadership implications of your areas of future growth (e.g., particular cultural/demographic groups you want to learn more about; reaction of colleagues to particular cultural/demographic groups).

_____

_____

_____

_____

Your responses to these writing activities are intended to support you in creating an intentional journey toward cultural proficiency. Keep your responses in mind as you read the next section that describes a planned path for your journey. In the last section of this chapter you are provided an opportunity to design and use benchmarks for your journey toward cultural proficiency.

YOUR AUTOBIOGRAPHY AND
DATA INFORM THE LEADERSHIP PLAN

In Chapter 3 you wrote and, most likely revised, your cultural autobiography. Earlier in this chapter you returned to Chapters 4, 5, and 6 and summarized and synthesized your learning from personal growth experiences and, then, you summarized your cross-cultural interviews. From these experiences you have developed an understanding of how and from whom you developed certain cross-cultural values and assumptions. Now that you know the foundation for your values and assumptions, you are well prepared to be specific in your areas of intended growth as a person, educator, and leader in diverse communities.

Table 7.2, The Journey From Cultural Precompetence to Cultural Proficiency illustrates intentional growth of a school leader. In this illustration, the leader has examined and decided what he needs to

Table 7.2   The Journey From Cultural Precompetence to Cultural Proficiency

	Cultural Precompetence	Cultural Competence	Cultural Proficiency
Descriptors	Learning*	Doing*	Achieving*
Culturally proficient leadership behaviors applied to the achievement issues of _____ (cultural/ demographic group) students	• The leader begins to "know what he doesn't know" about identified demographic groups of students. • The leader engages in her own learning about the cultures of the demographic groups and data that illustrates insufficiency on the part of the school.	• The leader collects data to inform new learning about the progress of demographic groups of students. • The leader initiates discussion and dialogue for purposes of analyzing disaggregated data.	• Data indicate student achievement is improving for all demographic groups. • The leader's commitment to social justice for demographic groups of students is evident.

Descriptors	Cultural Precompetence Learning*	Cultural Competence Doing*	Cultural Proficiency Achieving*
	• The leader learns **with** his colleagues, both those who are peer leaders and those peers he supervises. • The leader establishes, with colleagues, performance outcomes for students and selves.	• The leader uses data to select and implement strategies to better serve demographic groups of students' academic and social needs. • The leader monitors implementation of strategies for continuous improvement of students identified by demographic groups.	• The leader advocates for students identified as underserved and needing to be served differently. • The leader serves as mentor to those under-represented in the school and the profession. • The leader identifies her and the school's ongoing learning needs about demographic groups of students and continually views herself as recycling through the precompetence to competence to proficiency cycle

* Terminology added by our coauthor, Stephanie Graham, and her colleagues at the Los Angeles County Office of Education.

Table 7.3   My Journey From Cultural Precompetence to Cultural Proficiency

Descriptors	Cultural Precompetence	Cultural Competence	Cultural Proficiency
	Learning*	*Doing**	*Achieving**
Refer to your "areas of future growth" from earlier in this chapter and list key words: 1. 2. 3. 4. 5. Refer to the "leadership implications" from earlier in this chapter and fill in the blanks: I want to learn more about _____ (cultural group(s)) because _____	Upon considering the questions in the previous column, what do you want to learn?	Once you have learned, how will you use your new knowledge or skills?	What are the observable outcomes for: • you • your students • your colleagues • your school • the community you serve

* Terminology added by our coauthor, Stephanie Graham, and her colleagues at the Los Angeles County Office of Education.

learn, in what ways his learning informs what he is to do, and what he is to achieve.

You are now ready to develop your own plan. Using your notes from earlier in this chapter, select an area of cultural growth important to you. Use Table 7.3 to record what you want to learn, what you will do, and what you want to achieve. Column one guides you in identifying a cultural/demographic group about which you want to learn more. Column one also poses questions for you to consider. Columns two, three, and four are for you to record your responses in a manner that develops a plan of action.

Reflection

Like commencement, your journey has not ended—it has begun anew. How do you react to the work you are doing with this book? Please use the space below to record your thoughts, reactions, and feelings.

_____

_____

_____

_____

Educators and the Promise of Democracy **8**

Education is the most powerful weapon, which you can use to change the world.

—Nelson Mandela
(as cited in Anderson, p. 69)

GETTING CENTERED

In the first chapter of this book, we assumed you chose to read this book because you are an educator, a leader, and one who is interested in diversity and equity in our schools. Our schools are crucibles for our diverse society demonstrating that education is a right not a privilege. Together we have a role in making a vision of inclusive education accessible for all demographic groups of students. Think about your role as an educational leader, your response to activities in this book, and write in the space below what makes you hopeful.

_____

_____

_____

_____

Where do you go from here? Randy and Ray invited you to develop your own racial autobiography. We also invited you to explore what it takes to become culturally competent. As you travel on this journey, the next question to ask is, "so what?" What does it mean to discover who you are as a cultural being? What does it mean for the students you teach? What does it mean when you interact with your colleagues? What does it mean when you engage parents and community members?

Like commencement, the work is just beginning. Two recent experiences, one Ray's and one Randy's, illustrate the ongoing nature of our work.

RAY'S RECENT "SO WHAT" EXPERIENCE

Preston Wilcox, a community activist and champion of social justice, said to a group of us back in the '60s:

> I know that all of you can easily express love for and reach out and hug that little black, snotty nosed kid from Harlem. The question that you ultimately have to answer is can you reach above that kid and embrace his/her Mama with the same comfort and enthusiasm? For if you cannot, then you have not really embraced that kid because that kid is really his Mama. If you have concerns about her, then you really have concerns about him or her.

In order to teach all of our young people, we have to be able to see them and get to know them as they know us. Let us emphasize—*they get to know us because the things that all kids study most intensely are teachers.* Our students have a keen sense as to who we are and how we feel about them. They sense even those hidden biases that we may not even be in touch with. Ray recently had a teacher say to him, with great pride, "Someone asked me how many black kids I had in my class, and I told them I really didn't know because that's not how I see them." Ray's response to her was, "My five-year-old nephew just began kindergarten. When he came home after his first day there I asked him to tell me about his teacher. He simply responded, 'She's white.' I will be troubled if she does not see him as a black male."

Elementary schools are where the greatest cultural divide too frequently exists—the divide between European American female teachers and African American males. We only need to look at elementary suspension data, and the causes for suspensions to see a disproportionate rate of suspensions, mostly for disrespect. The issue of disrespect, when deconstructed too frequently, is a cultural clash between the student and the teacher, and the student always loses. So it is important that we as educators understand the implications that he sees skin color as being important enough to use it to describe her. I can only hope that she sees it as equally important and can use that awareness to positively motivate and educate him.

RANDY'S RECENT "SO WHAT" EXPERIENCE

I received a phone call a couple of years ago from the assistant principal of a large, comprehensive high school inviting me to provide a workshop for the teachers. He had heard of my work from a neighboring school district and he, his principal, and assistant superintendent liked the sound of "cultural proficiency" and thought this was what was needed at the school. He told me I would have two hours and would be working with about one hundred educators. My antennae rose immediately! I asked, "Is there an issue at the school?" What ensued was an engaging hour conversation with an administrator intent on doing good work for his teacher colleagues and his students.

It was late spring when the assistant principal and I had our conversation. The tale he began to unravel was familiar and has recurred across the country. The previous spring, gay and lesbian students were planning a commemoration of the National Day of Silence to protest sexual orientation bias. In response, a community group supported other students to counterprotest with disparaging verbal and print comments. The emerging conflict threw the school in to a tizzy. The protest and counterprotests occurred near the end of the school year and the educators were somewhat relieved that the summer break was about to begin. When school resumed in the autumn, the protests of the previous spring were not addressed. As early spring rolled around, it became apparent to school leaders that the protests were going to recur.

Once I knew the background to the issues, I asked, "What has been done since the protests of last spring?" The honest answer was that very little had been done. I asked, "Are you looking for a speaker to defuse the issue and to serve as a lightning rod for any disaffection?" The assistant principal demurred and, then, admitted it did sound like that was the task. I countered by suggesting that I come to the school and meet with a professional development committee comprised of teachers, all site administrators, and the assistant superintendent. I explained that my experience said the two-hour session had little chance of being successful and the school truly needed a comprehensive approach to an issue of equity. I offered to come at my own expense. It has been two years and I have yet to hear from the district. The issues have not abated.

LEARNING IS CONTINUOUS AND WITHIN

The common frame in each of these situations is the continuous learning process that must be in place in our schools. In each of our recent experiences is the opportunity for educators to take the bold step of looking inward to themselves and to their school and addressing inequities. The needed common denominator in each case is the willingness to make "undiscussables" visible.

So what, we ask again. There are three Johns who have tried to help us think about the "so what question." John Dewey challenged us when he posited:

> The aim of public education is to enable individuals to continue their education . . . [and] the object and reward of learning is continued capacity for growth. Now this idea cannot be applied to all members of society except where intercourse of man with man is mutual, and except where there is adequate provision of social habits and institutions by means of wide stimulation arising from equitably distributed interests. And this means a democratic society. (Dewey, 2006)

Unfortunately, our educational institutions have not fulfilled the vision that Dewey espoused. We have also failed to heed John Gardner (1961) who argued that the United States must strive for both excellence and equity at every level of our society. He so eloquently stated:

> We don't even know what skills may be needed in the years ahead. That is why we must train our young people in the fundamental fields of knowledge, and equip them to understand and cope with change. That is why we must give them the critical qualities of mind and durable qualities of character that will serve them in circumstances we cannot even predict. (p. 67)

Gardner's words ring as true today as they did more than forty-five years ago. I vividly remember debating in my education classes whether we could in reality have excellence and equity in our schooling processes. We encounter that same debate in education classes that I teach every day, and all evidence points to the fact that the issue is still unresolved.

The third John is Jonathan Kozol. He has been a determined crusader who constantly points out the inequities that are deeply rooted in our educational systems and throughout society. He documents case after case, example after example, of how we fail to provide equity in education and other aspects of our society for students of color and poor students. How we use slogans about "not throwing money at the problem," while we do not yet offer equal educational opportunities, facilities, instruction, and the notion of equity to these resources is seldom mentioned. We read *Death at an Early Age* and *Savage Inequalities* and have discussions about them, yet things remain status quo or fester and continue to get worse. In his *Letters to a Young Teacher* (2007), Kozol responds to the teacher's bewilderment of educational policy setting with this comment:

> While you were watching them you asked me whether anyone I know who's setting educational policy these days ever speaks about the sense of fun that children have, or ought to have, in public school or the excitement that they take when they examine interesting creatures such as beetle-bugs and ladybugs and other oddities of nature that they come upon—or even merely whether they are happy children and enjoy the hours they spend with us at school.
>
> The truth is that in all the documents I read that come from Washington or from the various state capitals, . . . , I never come on words such as "delight" or "joy" or "curiosity" or, for that matter, "kindness," "empathy," or "compassion for another child." (p. 99–100)

One teacher asked "Where do we start?" The size of the problem seems too large to get our arms around it; however, each of us has to decide if we are going to be part of the problem or part of the solution. We have invited you to get to know who you are and provided you with some tools to critically examine your school and your community. Of course, you first start with understanding yourself and how you view and interact with people who are different from you.

THE WILL AND SKILL OF THE CULTURALLY PROFICIENT LEADER

With this book we have sought to create a developmental approach to cross-cultural leadership development. Our cultural autobiographies were the first step in the process and enabled us to gain perspective on equity issues in education. The second step was to provide guidance for you, the reader, to understand from whom and how you developed values and embedded assumptions about people who are culturally different from you. The third step was to construct opportunities to interview people who hold these cultural differences so you could be intentional in your areas of intentional growth as a person and as a school leader. The fourth and final step was to have you construct a plan of action for moving from cultural precompetence to cultural proficiency.

From the activities integral to the four-step process outlined above, you have these awarenesses:

- Educators functioning at cultural competence are at the *here and now* stage of the change process. This educator (e.g., teacher, administrator, counselor, aide, custodian, office staff) is experienced as being *in the moment* in performing her professional practice in a manner that honors her students, their parents/guardians, their language, and their community. She is building educational programs with students' cultures as the foundation of their learning and development. Student success, by whatever measures employed, is central to her focus as a professional educator. Student success is her moral imperative.
- The culturally proficient educator is committed to life-long learning. He strives to understand his reactions to people culturally different from himself in order to recognize his values in action and the assumptions embedded in his actions. Knowing one's values and underlying assumptions is basic to being receptive to learning about people culturally different from you. It is at this moment that you are able to work with students and parents in ways that honor who they are, not trying to make them into images of you.
- The culturally proficient educator has internalized *advocacy* as a means of *social justice* for those historically underserved in our schools and related agencies.
- The culturally proficient educator is a mentor to those underserved in our schools and communities and to fellow educators in their journeys toward cross-cultural effectiveness.
- The culturally proficient educator uses the tools of cultural proficiency to address potential conflict between the cultures of our schools and of our diverse communities as a model of practice and *action.* The equity issues in our society speak to embracing advocacy at the heart of what we do as educators.

FINAL REFLECTION

It has been quite a journey! Together, we have revisited who we are and how we came to be in relation to our diverse country. We have examined our roles as educators and the plans we have to be even more effective with our students and communities. Please use the space below to record the reactions, feelings, thoughts, or questions that are with you now.

_____

_____

_____

_____

_____

_____

_____

_____

The final "so what" is the measure of your determination to join us in making a commitment to taking socially responsible action. In doing so, will you:

- adopt a moral position that all children and youth have the capacity to learn at high levels?
- make it your business to find ways to educate all children and youth to high levels?

It is for these last two bulleted statements that our occupation is referred to as a *profession*. A profession is characterized by requiring extensive education. The extensiveness of our education must begin, not end, with our university degrees. The culturally proficient educator uses his school and community as a veritable laboratory for his own lifelong learning in service of others. It is our journey together as a community of learners. Randy and Ray are pleased to have you as a fellow traveler on this journey.

It has been our pleasure to be with you on your journey. Accordingly, we would enjoy hearing from and learning with you. Please feel free to contact us.

—Raymond D. Terrell
terrelr@muohio.edu

—Randall B. Lindsey
randallblindsey@aol.com

Appendix A

Ray's Cultural Autobiography

EARLY FAMILY

I was the second child born to William Lester and Laura Lavada Terrell. I had three siblings, all girls—Gertrude who was six years older than me, Faithie who is eighteen months younger, and Irma who was six years younger. I have come to realize how the designation of spoiled might have been attributed to me. I was my mother's favorite which is often the case with African American women and their sons. Though I had many fights and arguments with my siblings, my three sisters also doted on me. They thought that it was special to have a brother. My sister, Faithie, who was closest to me in age, would often indicate that her big brother would beat someone up who was "messin'" with her. My father, of course, always took pride in starting a conversation about "My son." He had one sister and eight brothers, and he was the only one of his siblings to have a son. It was my responsibility to see that the Terrell name and lineage would be carried on. So, my place as special was established very early.

My father taught me to have great respect for women by example. As much as my mother and sisters doted on me, my father actively pampered my mom and his three daughters. He did have a "boys will be boys" attitude that allowed me to get away with a wide range of mischievous acts if he discovered them. My mom, on the other hand, seemed to find no humor in my many escapades, and she became the chief disciplinarian. I later found out that she was often amused by many of my antics, but she was afraid that the larger community, particularly the larger white community, would not see the humor and that punishment from those forces could prove to be lethal.

There was also a large extended family in and around our small community and the collective sense of family provided a great deal of support and self esteem. This support was important during a time when overt racism and segregation was so flagrant, and I was always made to feel special at home.

My mother worked as a domestic for one of the community's leading white families and my father was a laborer at a steel mill in a neighboring community. My parents' relationship was stable. Because both parents worked, it was my perception that we were fairly well off, a black family not experiencing any of the usual indicators of poverty . . . disconnected utilities, a lack of food, and we had one of the first televisions in our neighborhood. My mom had a fifth grade education and I discovered that she had difficulty reading when I brought her a note from high school and she had me read it to her. My dad had a sixth grade education but he was an avid reader and followed current events in the newspaper and by listening to daily newscasts.

The fact that they worked two very different jobs afforded them very different social perspectives and worldviews, and both of them freely shared their perspectives with me. As a domestic for a powerful family in the community, my mom viewed the world as a very dangerous place for African American males. She constantly admonished me to be sure to be polite and show deference to white people in order to avoid confrontations that could ultimately prove to be deadly. There was no one at my father's work place who had any community connections. He felt that he had a social responsibility to challenge the status quo around issues of social justice and constantly challenged the segregated school setting and other forms of local discrimination. It was confusing, to say the least, to constantly get input from such divergent points of view, while at the same time experience exclusion from local eateries, athletic facilities, and other public venues.

My father taught me how to identify and question level one issues. He was considered to be a radical for those times around local issues. I failed to grasp the breadth or depth of the scope of racism. Living in a very narrowly defined space and place and being internally focused, masked how racism negatively impacted the lives of everybody. I clearly had no notion that whites, though impacted differently, were also negatively affected by acquiring an inflated sense of privilege and entitlement.

My parents were very religious. My dad was a deacon in the local Baptist church and my mom sang in the choir. I joined the church when I was about ten-years-old. I also sang in the choir and served on the usher board. As I grew older, I developed my own philosophy of religion. I consider myself a very spiritual being, but I am skeptical of organized religions. I know that church and the interactions around them serve an essential purpose in the lives of many people. I also know that deep-rooted beliefs can also be a source of division between and among people.

I often wonder if it's possible to be a true believer of any form of religion and at the same time *value* those who hold totally different beliefs.

THE COMMUNITY

I was born in 1935 in Glendale, Ohio. It is interesting to reflect back as I have often done, and think about the fact that I grew up in a little village just north of Cincinnati, Ohio, which in fact was a plantation. In 1977, the United States Department of the Interior declared the community to be a National Historic Landmark District, and it has been designated as a local historic district since 1993. Many of the old homes have been renovated and restored and hold distinction as having historical relevance. Many of the current residents take great pride in living in a community with an impressive historical resumé, and they embrace this recognition as pleasant and quaint nostalgia. The "Negroes" who grew up and lived in my community experienced the legacy of the sometimes subtle, but more often blatant, racism that resulted in a different view of their life experiences in Glendale, and so began one saga of the great divide in black and white America that is rooted in periods of historic distrust, misunderstanding, and miscommunication. What is important about the saga is the extent that much of the reality of the fairly recent past that many want to dismiss as history—why don't they get over "it"—is still prevalent and raises barriers that prevent authentic black and white relationships from flourishing today. What is even more important is the impact that growing up in that community and in my family helped shape my racial identity and my sense of race and place as making significant, indelible impressions on me. It also inspires me to write in tandem with my friend and colleague about growing up separate and unequal in the eyes of many and still find ways of resistance, resilience, and finally reconciliation internally and externally.

Why I call the Glendale of the '40s, '50s, and '60s a plantation is because in some of its official documents, the community leaders codified the practices that had always existed in Glendale by declaring that the village would always have a greenbelt, have no industry, and maintain a small community of Negroes who would serve as domestic help for the rest of the community. Now while there was no cotton to be picked in Glendale, there were clear markers established that clarified ones position as it was related to race and place.

The majority of the Negro population resided in the northwest section of the community. There was a small subdivision in the northeast side of the railroad tracks and a small settlement on the southeast side of the tracks. The majority of the people of "substance" lived in the southwest section of the village, west of the railroad tracks. There were large estates in this area that housed owners and executives of Proctor and Gamble, some Cincinnati banking interests, lawyers from major downtown firms, and owners of other corporations in surrounding communities. There were three primary institutions in the Negro community, Mt. Zion Baptist

Church, Quinn Chapel African Methodist Episcopal Church, and Eckstein School, which was a four room, Grade 1–8 elementary school with two grade levels in each of the four rooms.

There was an early experience with ableness that had a profound effect on me. We had a cousin named Sonny. Sonny was physically deformed with both his hands and feet being webbed, his head being pointed and his eyes being enlarged. He operated mentally at the level of an eight-year-old. Sonny was institutionalized in a state hospital, but he was allowed home visits. When he came to stay with us for two or three two-week visits a year, we shared a bedroom because I was the only boy in the house. The visits occurred for me between the ages of five and fifteen before Sonny died.

At first all of my friends were afraid of Sonny because of the way that he looked and talked, and they would make fun of him. I knew Sonny as a warm, gentle, caring person who loved baseball, especially the Cincinnati Reds. He knew statistics, batting averages, players, and histories. We listened to every game on the radio when he visited. He also liked to do little favors for anyone in the house. I finally had to confront some of my friends and ended one friendship because she refused to accept Sonny. This living experience provided me with insights into how persons could be cruel to someone who was physically and mentally disabled. It was clear to me that this was a form of discrimination based on appearances and a basic ignorance of the person that Sonny was. It was also clear to me that this was a form of bias and discrimination that I always committed to confronting and changing.

THE SCHOOL EXPERIENCE

There was another school in the village. We called it the Congress Avenue School. It served as the first twelfth grade school for white residents. The Negroes who made it to high school also attended the high school portion of the Congress Avenue School. The above reference to "those who made it" to the high school refers to the fact that the Eckstein School, the school for Negroes in Glendale, served a highly sophisticated function of sorting and determining who would get passage to move on to Glendale High School. The clear indicators of this process were marked by the number of my sixth grade classmates who were fifteen, sixteen, and even seventeen years old, and a process of repeated retention until some simply dropped out. In fact, there was a practice implemented in my seventh/eighth-grade classroom where the principal, who lived in the house next-door to the school, would call roll in the morning and assign domestic work and yard work to half of my class and indicate that they would be pursuing careers as domestics and yard boys in the near future and needed to hone those skills. The rest of us would remain and engage in academic pursuits.

The total experience at Glendale High School is interesting to look back on as a current day educator. The school population was very small. There were eighteen students in my graduating class, four African Americans. The athletic activities were desegregated; however all social activity was segregated, at least until after I had graduated. There were separate dances and the Negro prom was always held in the gym back at Eckstein School. Because some of the children of the upper middle class attended high school there, we had features like tea dances on Thursday afternoons where we all went to the gym to learn how to pour tea, hold our cup and saucer properly while eating scones and crumpets, and how to dance the two step and the box step. This activity was abruptly terminated when one of my classmates, an African American male, asked one of the white girls to dance with him and she accepted—"whoa," no more tea dances.

The issue of language became a major factor in helping to shape my racial identity. I entered high school with Ebonics as my primary language. The submersion into an environment where "standard English" was the coin of the realm was a real shock. The teachers at Eckstein had provided me with an excellent basis for understanding the context and written forms of "standard English." However, my verbal communications were all routinely done in Ebonics, the language spoken by everyone at home and in my neighborhood. As I began to develop spoken "standard" fluency, I was ridiculed by friends and family as, "There go Raymond talkin' proper" and "There go Raymond talkin' like white folks." I was in a real state of cultural confusion and experiencing high degrees of marginality—not fitting in or being totally accepted by either the white students nor my African American family or peers.

There was one factor when viewed through my current day eyes as an educator I find to be most interesting. Even though all of the high school teachers were white, contrary to much of the research around expectations, all of the teachers made demands and indicated that they expected high achievement from all students present including the Negro students. In many ways, those of us who were lucky enough to come out the back end of the sorting machine received an education akin to the opportunity that is now afforded to students in elite private schools. Class size was small and the range of course offerings was fairly broad, including a number of foreign languages, mathematics through trigonometry, and science through chemistry and physics. Charles Warman, a social studies teacher, said to me one day, "You are smart and capable of being anything that you want to be." That was a message that the African American teachers had given me all through my Eckstein experience, and I had, in fact, been double promoted and spent only one year in the seventh/eighth grade room before moving on to high school. However, in the face of much of the racism that surrounded me in the high school and the larger community, I had begun to lose my compass and the struggle of identity was constantly being challenged.

One notable issue of segregation revolved around the swimming pool. Negroes were allowed to swim one day per week, on Mondays. There were three sessions, one from 10:00–12:00 in the morning, an afternoon session from 3:00–4:00 and an evening session from 7:00–8:00. It was important that you swim very fast in the evening session because the pool was being drained to be cleaned and refilled for the rest of the community to use for the next six days.

Each year, students who could afford it took a trip, year one to Washington, DC, year two to Chicago, year three to New York City, and year four a bus to Detroit where we boarded a boat and cruised up Lake Erie to Niagara Falls. Because I worked as a yard boy and cut grass and raked leaves at some of the local mansions, I was able to save enough to make the trip all four years. Yet, again, on our way to Washington, DC, our great nation's capital, we were forced to dine in separate facilities at our lunch stop in West Virginia.

Thankfully, high school graduation finally came and I decided that I needed to flee the local oppression. Six days later I enlisted in the U. S. Navy. Certainly, if I wore the uniform of one of the services of this great country, I would instantly receive the respect that I thought I was due as a citizen. Little did I know or anticipate the racism that I would encounter as I ventured into the military and the larger society.

THE MILITARY EXPERIENCE

In 1952, the Navy was making moves to open opportunities to Negro sailors beyond the service areas as steward mates and deckhands. I became a hospital corpsman. I was the only black in my training and the only black in my working unit. While stationed at the naval hospital at Bainbridge, Maryland, I experienced a traumatic identity crisis. All of my informal activities were with work colleagues who were white, most of them from New York and New Jersey with attitudes a bit more liberal than other whites that I had encountered. However, when we would attempt to go out to dinner or to a movie in the local area, including Baltimore and Washington, DC, we would be told that I either could not be admitted to eat at all or, if I chose to stay, that I would have to eat in a separate area. My white colleagues always refused service in these places and we started to take liberty by taking a train to Philadelphia or New York City where we could be served together. This process worked so well that I started to believe that I had the same status as my white colleagues.

It was at the hospital that I experienced my most shocking two experiences with racism and again one experience that gave me hope of redemption and kept me from painting all whites as my enemy. The first incident occurred when I was pulling duty in the emergency room. An African American male arrived in an ambulance and he was pronounced dead on arrival. I discovered that he had slipped under a railroad car at the local train station and his leg had been severed. He was initially taken to two local hospitals and been refused admission because he was black.

The ambulance driver eventually brought him to the naval hospital, but too late; he had bled to death. I had never experienced anyone who had lost their life just because they were black. I was in a real state of turmoil, despair, and total confusion.

My situation became even more problematic a week later. My regular assignment was in the hospital laboratory. One night while standing watch I was called at 2:00 in the morning to go and draw blood and do a type and cross match to set up a transfusion for a white, female dependent who had just given birth and lost a lot of blood in the process. I completed my task and the next morning I was called into the office of the hospital administrator. He informed me that the woman whose blood I had drawn had accused me of raping her while I was in the room alone with her. I was devastated and totally petrified with fear. I knew of no circumstance where such a charge, when made by a white woman against an African American, had ever been disbelieved, especially when there were no witnesses present. The doctor, who served as the director of the laboratory and my immediate boss, spoke and said, "The charges are bullshit." The administrator asked the doctor if an investigation had been completed? The doctor said, "No, and we aren't going to do one. I know this man well enough to know that he is not capable of such an act."

I had never had a white male step up and defend me unconditionally before. I had now experienced an all-time low and a major spiritual pick-me-up in a very short period of time. However, I still was not about to be open and trusting around white people again. Life and death based on racism became a real possibility in my life space. It was no longer something that I read about or heard people discuss. What I failed to realize, even as an eighteen-year-old, was how permanent this reality would become as it continued to raise its ugly head again and again across my lifetime, up to and including this very day. What I also failed to realize was how my reality was to be so poorly understood, dismissed, and often distorted by many whites that I encountered. I began to realize that simply being white carried with it some fundamental privileges that I as an African American male would never experience, and how important my constant awareness of the color of my skin was to day-to-day emotional, psychological, and physical health and sanity.

The military was also a time when I first encountered a cultural reality that had never been discussed in my small hometown. I had no knowledge or experience with anyone who was homosexual. The lack of knowledge also meant that I had no feelings of bias for different sexual orientations. One of my shipmates "hit" on me one day. I didn't at first realize what he was asking me. He explained the attraction that he felt for me and how he wished to express his affection. I was curious, and he was willing to engage in an ongoing discussion explaining his feelings, when he was aware of them, and how natural they were for him. He introduced me to other gay men that he knew and a lesbian couple who shared an apartment in Long Beach. I became an adopted member in the community. While there were other shipmates who then began to believe that I might be homosexual, I was always comfortable enough with myself to not be threatened.

As an African American, I knew what it was like to be looked down on in this society. I also knew, that while I shared being shunned and oppressed by large segments of the society with my new friends in this community, they were all white and until they chose to come out, there were still privileges that they enjoyed that I did not. One of the real rewards for me in these relationships was that through dialogue and inter-action, we developed awareness about their whiteness and the difference in forms of oppressions. Once we worked through those issues, the "oppression Olympics" came to an end. While both groups were oppressed, systemic, institutional racism was deeply rooted in the every-day way of life in America.

THE COLLEGE EXPERIENCE

Two weeks after being discharged from the navy I used the G. I. Bill and enrolled at Miami University in Oxford, Ohio, with hopes of pursuing psychology as my major. I was twenty-one-years-old with three and a half years of naval service. My classmates were eighteen-years-old, over-whelmingly white, and socioeconomically mostly upper middle-upper class. I stayed for a semester and a half at the university before dropping out. There were two major factors that influenced my decision. The first was the feeling of racial and socioeconomic isolation. I spent most of the time when I was in the navy in racial isolation because of my work station. However, most of the whites in that environment were at the same or even a lower socioeconomic background than mine. The university provided me my first experience with persons near my age who openly expressed and acted from positions of white, male, rich entitlement.

I was initially intimidated by the fact that my classmates were all freshly out of high school with great study habits and that they may have been smarter than me. After a few weeks of class, this notion was dis-missed and replaced by my new attitude questioning how folks who were so shallow could be admitted to the university. I found that I could com-pete academically without breaking a sweat. There was a small but tight knit group of African Americans on campus and that provided some social outlets, but being the only person of color in class after class and being expected to be the Negro expert wore thin very quickly.

Finally, there was a defining incident that drove me from the univer-sity. While sitting in the lounge in my dorm one evening, the newspaper that I was reading suddenly went up in flames. There was then a group of six of my dorm mates who were beside themselves with laughter. I threw the paper on the floor and stomped it out and then pushed the person who was closest to me and he stumbled and fell. I then reported the incident to the resident assistant. They convened a hearing and the final conclusion was that I, as a more mature, navy veteran, should have been able to conduct myself in a more prudent manner, and because of my training, I could have seriously hurt one of the "kids," all of whom were just having some fun. It became very clear to me that Miami University was not the place for me, so I dropped out, and moved to California where I thought that people would be more socially liberal.

BETWEEN COLLEGES EXPERIENCES

I took a job as a clerk in the Santa Monica post office. I discovered that place didn't make a lot of difference when it came to race. Southern Californians were more sophisticated in their racist expressions and actions, however, slights and insults were an everyday reality. After a year and a half, I was told that my father had a serious illness and I applied for and received a transfer to the Cincinnati post office. The transfer was granted and I returned home to Glendale, Ohio. It proved to be one of the best moves that I ever made. I met and married Eloise Kemp and she has been a constant source of grounding aside from the constant tender, loving support that she has used to help me understand who I am. Ellie and I had a son, William Harvey, and she then began to encourage me to return to school. She had grown up as a Catholic and attended Our Lady of Mercy High School. Ellie had encountered a priest, Father McCarthy, who was a faculty member at Xavier University in Cincinnati. She brought the two of us together, and the two of them encouraged me to enroll at Xavier. I worked the midnight shift at the post office, and attended Xavier during the day. During my junior year, Ellie and I had our second child, a daughter, Dina Celeste.

The Xavier College Experience

Father McCarthy served as a mentor for me through my entire Xavier experience. He was the most positive and consistent white male to have an impact on me. One of the requirements of all Xavier students was to have a minor in philosophy. It was through my ethics class and my reading of many of the great philosophers that I began to seriously confront issues of social justice and be able to develop a voice that allowed me to begin to address the issues strategically. I had learned how to identify and complain about the issues. I had not developed an understanding of how they evolved, festered, and were perpetuated, therefore, rendering many of my proposed solutions ineffective. Aside from the general classroom assignments and discussions, Father McCarthy held special informal discussion groups on a regular basis with me and a few of the other African American students at Xavier. He challenged us to think deeply about the issues of racism and poverty and constantly insisted that we always ask over and over again "Why?" if were ever to develop full understanding.

The Princeton Experience

With a lot of encouragement, support, and insistence from Ellie— especially when I hit those low periods and wanted to drop out again—I finally earned my bachelor's degree with a major in English and a minor in education. Armed with all of my newfound knowledge and credentials, I was offered a job in the Princeton City School District. The Princeton district was a consolidated district that included the village of Glendale, my old district, and several other surrounding communities. Many of the teachers and administrators in the district were persons who had taught me as a youngster. It was interesting to try to return home again to my school community.

The district had a student population that was 10 percent African American and 90 percent European American. It was, at the secondary level, one of the most desegregated suburban districts in the area. The elementary schools were all local community schools. Five of the elementary schools were populated by white students and three contained desegregated populations. I taught English at the high school my first year and then was moved to the junior school my second year where I also taught English. The junior school (Grades 7 and 8) was the place where all of the students came together for the first time and issues of race and conflict emerged. My placement there, aside from teaching English, was to assist the administration with helping the students who came into this new totally desegregated setting make the transition more smoothly. I spent three years at the junior school where I also coached track, basketball, and flag football teams.

After college graduation, I immediately pursued my master's degree and administrative credential at Xavier. The Woodlawn community was the most desegregated community in the district. The community had been targeted by realtors and banking institutions for block busting techniques that saw the racial make-up change from about 10 percent African American to more than 50 percent African American in a very short time period. I lived in the Woodlawn community and served on the community's village council and eventually became vice-mayor. The community's elementary school was located on two campuses about a half mile apart. One building housed students in grades K-3 and the other building served the Grade 4–6 population.

At the end of my third year at the junior school, the superintendent called me to a meeting to ask if I was willing to become a principal at the 4–6 building. I agreed to take the position, and then had a call two days later to meet again with the superintendent. He informed me that the white male who had tried to cover both buildings, but who now would only have the K-3 building, had come in and complained that the move would be seen as a demotion for him, and that I should be designated as an assistant principal. I responded that to retract the offer would diminish my status in the eyes of the school faculty and the community. We settled on a compromise that named us as coprincipals of Woodlawn Schools with the two of us having an understanding that we ran total autonomous operations in each of our buildings.

In the middle of my first year as principal, I was offered a fellowship from the C.S. Mott Foundation to pursue a doctorate at Wayne State University in Detroit, Michigan. I consulted with my superintendent and he indicated that he had great future plans for me in the district and he wholeheartedly supported the move. He, in fact, offered me a sabbatical, and paid me one half of my salary for the year that I was away to complete the coursework with a commitment that I would return to the district for at least two years. So, it was off to graduate school.

The Wayne State Experience

The Mott Fellowship program had a mission of spreading the philosophy of community education to a national audience. The concept was to develop ways to maximize partnerships between schools, their students and families, and the other governmental entities. It brought together a cohort of forty graduate students—ten doctoral students at each Wayne State, Michigan State, the University of Michigan, and Western Michigan and ten students seeking masters' degrees at Eastern Michigan and Central Michigan. We did our classroom work at our respective universities from Monday-Thursday and then we met on Fridays as a total group for colloquia and dialogue sessions with notable educators from all across the country. During our second semester, we were all scheduled to do an internship, and I was paired with a principal, Dr. Kenneth Fish, at Flint, Michigan's Northwestern High School. That relationship proved to be extremely beneficial to me. The year was 1970 and schools all across the country were experiencing disruptions and sit ins led by African American students who were demanding that our culture be included in curriculum and that teachers be taught to be more sensitive to the racial and cultural differences that students brought to school.

Northwestern High School was a school that had a growing black student population and had experienced unrest in the previous school year. Ken Fish had received a grant and had studied the disruptions that were occurring across the country, and he had developed a reputation as a national expert on conflicts that arise in desegregating schools. His reputation was a major factor in his selection as the principal at Northwestern. During my third week on the job, the African American students staged a sit in and demonstration in the auditorium. I accompanied Ken to the auditorium and we listened as the student leaders made a series of speeches identifying a series of wrongs at the school. Ken then took the stage and indicated that he heard their complaints, but he wanted them to know that as far as their demands, power did not concede anything unless there were real challenging demands. He and I then held a seminar on power and how it worked. The students met two more times and constructed and won concessions on a list to ten demands. The school became peaceful, curricular changes were started, and an ongoing staff development process was put into place.

One day in early May of 1970, Ken and I were in his office discussing how well things were going at the school when he took a phone call. It was a professor at Southwest Missouri State College who had a federal grant to work with school personnel from a large number of schools in that area of the country that were experiencing difficulties resolving conflicts similar to those that we had at Northwestern. They wanted Ken to come and conduct an all day workshop in early June. Ken checked his calendar and indicated that he was booked at the time that they wanted him, and then he said, "I know that you want my expertise and I'm sorry that I can't come, but I have sitting in my office right now, the second most knowledgeable and skilled person in the country about these issues." I had never conducted a workshop of any kind and never spoken to an audience larger than the ten teachers that I had at Woodlawn School. I felt like a bird that was being pushed out of a nest without ever having a flying lesson. As he helped me design the workshop, Ken continued to build my confidence and insisted that it would be "a piece of cake."

THE WORKSHOP

I was on my way to my first paid consultancy. Ken insisted that I be paid the same amount that they would have paid him, even though I had not published a book on the issues as he had done, nor did I have the status of being titled as "doctor." The workshop proved to be quite a success. I had a four-hour wait before my plane was to depart and return me to Cincinnati. They assigned an African American principal from a local school to take me back to the airport. He indicated that he was really into the issues as I had presented during the workshop and wanted to know if we could talk about them over a beer in much greater depth. I was delighted at the prospect. He drove to a local grocery store and bought a six pack of beer and began to drive out of town. I asked where we were going, and he indicated that it was not safe to publicly discuss such issues, so we ended up in the woods, sitting on the banks of the Mississippi River talking school desegregation and racial conflicts in those settings. Scary!

1970 AND BEYOND

It was 1970 when three additional white males would make significant impressions in my life space.

The Lincoln Heights Merger

There were major events occurring in my old school district while I was away. In May, my superintendent called for me to attend another meeting. He informed me that our district was taking in Lincoln Heights School District, a neighboring district, through a state supervised merger process. The neighboring district was rated as the poorest district in the state while our district was rated as the second wealthiest district in the state. The district had a 100 percent African American student population. Our district's profile went from 10 percent African American to 30 percent African American overnight. The high school and the junior school both experienced the increase in black students. The elementary schools, because they were community schools, had no changes, including Lincoln Heights Elementary which remained 100 percent black.

The superintendent then offered me an assistant superintendent position to help facilitate the merger process with a special focus on work with community groups and providing staff development for the faculty. This position began an unbelievable roller coaster ride. There were incidents of racial conflict at the high school that were marked by the local police force wanting to enter the building and crack heads. We were able to resist that pressure. There was a bus strike caused by a group of drivers who didn't want to drive the rowdy black students from Lincoln Heights. On the second morning of the strike, one of my jobs as an administrator was to read a court order to the pickets, who were blocking the buses that were rolling, to move aside and allow the buses to proceed. I was assaulted by the pickets and beaten about the head and ears with their picket signs while being told that Martin Luther King Jr. would be ashamed of me for crossing a picket line, even one that was constructed to discriminate against black children.

Issue of the Doctoral Dissertation

When I entered the doctoral program at Wayne State University, Dr. Duane Peterson had asked me if he could be my dissertation advisor and I consented. I had completed all of my coursework and had gathered all of my data for my dissertation while interning at Northwestern. The dissertation was to be titled, "The Anatomy of an Interracial High School." Having been recently promoted to the Assistant Superintendent position and being immersed in all of the issues surrounding the new merger, I decided that I didn't need to write the dissertation. I was very comfortable with the thought of being a doctoral candidate, and completion of the dissertation and actual doctorate was not that significant for me. Duane would not hear of it. He called my house and my office on what seemed like a weekly basis. He finally quit talking to me and began to communicate with my wife because he determined that she might have more influence over me. He even suggested that she might move my sleeping quarters out of our bedroom to the sofa in the family room until I began to write the dissertation. Ultimately, it was a combination of Duane and Ellie's constant nagging that pressured me to finish my dissertation. I have since learned that many faculty members are too frequently unavailable to their dissertation advisees and certainly most do not provide long distance pressure for them to succeed for two years. Thanks to Duane and the completion of the doctorate, an entire world of other opportunities opened up for me about which I was totally unaware.

The Ray and Randy Merger

While coordinating efforts to facilitate the school district's merger, we received a U. S. Department of Education Title IV grant that was designed to help school districts deal with issues, concerns, and problems related to school desegregation. One of the conditions for receiving the grant was that the district would have a representative participate in a one-week training that was to be conducted in Hartford, Connecticut. I arrived at the training site to discover that there were going to be forty persons trained across the country. We would each be designated with the title, "Advisory Specialist," armed with knowledge and skills to address issues incident to desegregation. There was an underlying assumption that we would form a national network so that we could communicate with each other and provide support, insight, and wisdom based on our varied experiences.

One of my colleagues who attended the training session was a white male, Randall Lindsey, who was working with the desegregation process in Kankakee, Illinois. I didn't realize at the time that this meeting was destined to turn into a thirty-five year partnership and ultimately a deep and abiding friendship. After the first day of training, Randy and I, while debriefing, had come to the same conclusion. The first day's training had been boring and not very informative. During our discussion, we decided that if we had to stay away from home for four more days in this setting, rather than simply complaining, we would take shared responsibility of pushing issues, raising questions, and posing different approaches to what the Hartford training team had proposed. We, in a word, took over the agenda for the next four days and turned what had started out to be a disaster into a successful and productive week for all of the participants. During our discussion, I was impressed with the commitment that Randy had related to the issue of obtaining equity for black youngsters in school. He also could say the word "racism" and not turn his head or divert his eyes from me. We both later came to understand that while we were ahead of the curve of many of our contemporaries, we had still just barely scratched the surface of the complexities related to racism and other "isms" that impact the lives of all of us.

In order to support the training needs of other district personnel, the superintendent had also contracted with a group of psychologists from the University of Cincinnati to provide sensitivity training for the district's administrative team. We scheduled a weekend retreat with this training team and all twenty district administrators including the new administrators from Lincoln Heights. The superintendent, for some reason, did not attend. After the first day's activities were completed, and we were taking a break before dinner, one of the training team's facilitators broke out a bottle of scotch whiskey and indicated that anyone who chose to was more than welcome to have a drink. One of the administrators indicated that he had a preference for beer and a group of three of them went to a local liquor store and purchased a case of beer. During the course of the evening, we engaged in debate and discussion about how best to address the needs of the new students from Lincoln Heights and how the roles of the Lincoln Heights administrators would be defined. As a part of the merger agreement, the superintendent of Lincoln Heights was provided an assistant superintendent position. Bob Lucas did not want two superintendents in his district.

The next morning, the training team had us participate in an activity that explored the issues of race and power. That was then followed by an activity that divided us into two caucus groups, one with all of the black administrators and one with all of the white administrators. One outcome of the black caucus dealt with the fact that there was an inordinate power differential between the black and white administrators, and that it would be my responsibility because of my history and close relationship with Lucas to take the lead as the primary advocate and broker for positions and points of view on behalf of black faculty, staff, students, and community. Some of the white administrators became secretly hostile to this idea and in a staff meeting told Lucas, "Terrell took us off to the woods on the retreat, plied us with liquor, made us confess that we were all racist, and established an imperial superintendency." Lucas and I had an in-depth discussion about the retreat and in the end, he fired the black and white males on the team and hired the white female to a permanent position. He assigned her to work with me on developing an in-house staff development unit to work on sensitivity and cultural awareness activities that would meet the commitment that we had made under our Title IV grant.

The team that I hired included one black male who had been in the Lincoln Heights system, a white male who had been a colleague in my doctoral program, a black male who was a new graduate from Kentucky State College, and a black male who had been a counselor in the district. I still had one position to fill when I got a phone call from Randy Lindsey explaining that he had been summarily fired from his position in Kankakee for pushing too hard to create some equity for students in his district. I got approval from Lucas and hired him immediately to complete my team. Each member of the team had primary responsibility for facilitating information and training school personnel and community members in two buildings. We met as a total group to also discuss what training was needed on a district-wide basis and designed a number of workshops and hired national consultants who offered insights on how to create curriculum and use pedagogical approaches to serve Princeton's new population.

There were two major and many lesser factors that we all missed. We were not fully prepared for the level of resistance from school staff and community members. We also were very naive about how power operated in a racialized environment. We thought that by providing enough information, people would simply change their attitudes and all would be right with the world. The high school was experiencing conflicts between black and white students and there were a growing number of suspensions, particularly among black males. I then took a position with Lucas that these issues would continue and be exacerbated by the fact that the district insisted on maintaining neighborhood elementary schools that were de facto segregated, and that once together at the junior high school the prior conditions set up conditions for cultural misunderstanding, hostility, and conflict. I proposed that we should consider busing students between two white elementary schools and Lincoln Heights Elementary in order to establish earlier cross-cultural contact, and also implement intensive training to improve faculty effectiveness in working in desegregated settings. Lucas agreed that the idea had some merit, but he contended that the white communities were not ready for such a move. It was my position that they would never be ready for such a move if left to their own devices. (Parenthetically, the same issue was raised in 2003 and the local board again opted to build eight new elementary buildings in local communities maintaining a continued form of racial and socioeconomic apartheid within the Princeton City School District.)

I felt very strongly about my position and continued to argue it with Lucas. At the end of the 1972 school year, he "promoted" me to a newly created position of Assistant Superintendent for Community Affairs, offered me a substantive pay raise, but took away all of my staff and responsibility for overseeing equity issues. I was essentially provided a new title while being stripped of all line of authority. It was clear to me that I was no longer going to be able to shape much of the Princeton equity agenda. At this time, I decided that I needed a change of scenery. I was saddened by this reality because the long hours and weekends that the team and I spent working, planning, dialoguing, and bonding were to be lost.

Along the way, I had developed an especially close relationship with Randy. He and I had built on the relationship that we had established at the Hartford training activity. We were both passionate and strident advocates for desegregating schools using processes that ensured that the burden of movement did not fall disproportionately on any one group, and that the teachers who worked in desegregated schools were provided with curricular materials and cultural sensitivity that would allow them to interact effectively with black students. At that time and place, the only equity issue that we perceived revolved around issues of race. That was the primary source of conflict and miseducation in our environment. It was an encounter with Dr. Barbara Sizemore in 1972 that raised gender equity issues on my radar scope.

Based on a good deal of reading, research, and personal experiences, our team formed an independent consultant company, Interracial Interactions Incorporated (III). We began to offer services to other school districts involved in desegregation activities. While working together in our planning processes, it became clear to Randy that as a white male, he was a recipient of status and other privileges that can be accrued in our society simply because of the intersection of his race and gender. While his background was basically Appalachian, as long as he did not reflect those early beginnings by using Appalachian speech, he could "pass" for any upwardly mobile white male. Not only was he a white male, he was also tall, handsome, exceptionally articulate, and appeared visually to be the "all American boy." Neither of us had experienced an extended time period when two individuals, one black and one white, spent as much time together both inside the workplace and outside of the workplace in social settings (restaurants, bars, theaters, etc.) and working as a black/white consulting team addressing issues of race and desegregation.

As we traveled about, we became aware of how strange our relationship and personal interactions were seen and responded to by many others. We carefully scripted the various roles that each of us would play, depending on the audience to be served, when we consulted and when we did staff development within the district. It came through with a great deal of clarity that would turn an audience completely off if uttered by me and vice versa. If the audience was predominately white and I said anything about racism, eyes glazed over, ears slammed shut, and the audience became a sea of deep sighs and rolling eyes. Randy's definitions and explanation of racism and how he participated in the process were, at least, listened to. On the other hand, any time he tried to explain any productive interactions that he had experienced working with black students was summarily dismissed as impossible. There could be no way that he could possibly understand any of the realities that black students faced in their school settings. The respect and insights that Randy and I began to develop and the level of trust and openness that we obtained, led us to countless hours of discussion, debate, and examination of motives and perspectives that each of us brought to the table.

I was chided by many of my colleagues to be careful and not allow myself to be misused by a white boy. What evolved, however, was not just a discussion about issues of equity; our relationship developed into one where we also began to share our most intimate personal issues. It was at this level that the relationship began to move from one of colleagues who mutually respected one another to one of deep affection, love, and friendship. It became apparent over time that Randy and I would do anything legal and perhaps illegal to assist one another. I was clear that if I needed anything at all, material or spiritual, Randy would willingly provide it and I would do the same for him. My needing to leave the district for what I saw as an ethical position was lamented but understood and supported by Randy. So, it was off to Texas A & M University to assume a position in the department of educational administration. This move was made possible because my dissertation advisor and my wife had pushed me to complete the doctorate degree. Randy helped me make the physical move to College Station, Texas.

I was the first black faculty member hired in my department at A & M. I might have been the first black faculty member hired at the university. If there were others there, they were kept a well-hidden secret. Ellie and our children were warmly greeted by the university community and our neighbors in the apartment complex where we lived. In fact, we were greeted and embraced by the total community and afforded almost a celebrity status not afforded any other new hire that year. There were newspaper articles and television interviews done about our arrival. Ellie was invited to join a social club that had never been integrated, and offered an opportunity by a major clothing store to do modeling.

There was a real push to make us feel very "special." However, there were a few incidents, inside the university and some significant others in the broader Texas community, that caused me to make a move after spending just one year at A & M. It should be noted first, that as a product of the midwest, primarily Ohio and Michigan, I had never personally encountered any one who was Hispanic, and I was totally unaware that across Texas, Hispanics were afforded second class status in much the same way that blacks were where I came from. I became aware of negative judgments that were based on skin color and Ebonics, so my Texas experience taught me that the issues of national origin and any language other than "standard English" were also relegated to the margin. It was common to hear demands that Hispanics be forbidden to speak Spanish because whites and even some blacks were concerned that they might be talking about them or making fun of them.

The two incidents inside the academy came about when one of my new colleagues said to me after I had been there about six weeks, "You know, if we could find another one just like you, we would hire him tomorrow." He had no sense that such a statement was offensive and when I confronted him he indicated that he meant to be complimentary. I explained to him that I would always be "just another one of them," and that I was "just another one of them" until he thought that he knew me fairly well. In terms of racial identity, there are things that you know instinctively, but until they are driven home by experience, you tend to maintain a certain level of denial. This incident had me fully realize that I would always have two very distinct but intertwined identities. I would always be an individual with all of my knowledge, abilities, values, beliefs, and behaviors, but to most people I would also always be "just another one of them," until I somehow proved to be "different from the rest of them."

The second incident occurred about six months into my stay. The dean of the college called me to a meeting and indicated that it was time for me to consider purchasing a residence and moving out of the apartment complex where my family and I were living. He indicated that he was on the board of directors of the local bank. He said that I should just look around the community, pick out a house, and I would be assured of funding by the bank. I thanked him and got up to leave the room when he said, "Oh, by the way, you can look in any part of the community for a house; you won't be restricted to the colored section." The combination of struggling with being "just another one of them," and being offered special treatment that would separate me from the "rest of them" created such a real internal conflict. This was compounded by the fact that my family had developed a close relationship with one other African American family in the community. They had shared with us the level of resentment that many other blacks felt because the new comers arrived in town and were receiving better treatment than old line residents had ever received. It also let me decipher the nebulous invitations that we would get from black families when we attended church in the community in the form of, "you all come on by for dinner some time," never followed up with any specificity as to where or when that would be possible. We were being isolated and insulated from the local black community. I had a long discussion with my wife about the various forms of special treatment that she, our kids, and I were receiving in this place and we decided that it could become seductive in that we could begin to believe that we were different from "the rest of them." We saw it particularly dangerous for our two children.

At the same time, I had three incidents on Texas highways that kept me aware of being "just another one of them." We drove to Cincinnati over the Christmas holidays, and while driving back, three white men in a pick-up truck deliberately tried to run our car off the road. I was driving at about 60 mph when they passed me, and cut in very sharply causing me to have to apply my brakes very hard. Just a coincidence? They waited up the road until we had passed them and repeated this maneuver twice more, all the while very visibly laughing at our collective distress.

The second time occurred when I was driving to teach my off-campus class in San Angelo, a six-hour drive that I was to make every week. A car made a left hand turn in front of me causing a collision. The driver of the car and I were exchanging information when a pick-up truck with a gun rack arrived with three young men in it. They got out of the truck and asked, "Mr. Waters, can we do anything to help you with your problem?" I spoke up and simply said, "It would be helpful if someone could summon a Ranger." The spokesman for the group then said to me, "You are the problem that we are talking about." Thankfully, Mr. Waters said "No, just see if you can get a Ranger." Very, very scary.

After the wreck, the university decided that I should drive an official station wagon to my teaching station. The first day out, I stopped in Brady, Texas, for gas and a group of men who were hanging around the gas station all came out, walked around the station wagon, noting the logo on the door, and then began to question me about who I was and where I was going. I explained the situation, they filled my gas tank, and sent me on my way. I decided that, since I was going to have to make this trip on a weekly basis, I did not want to have to make explanation at gas stations all across Texas, so I decided to purchase gas at this same station on each trip. On my last trip out, I pulled into the station and the attendant came out and said, "Filler up as usual?" I responded, in the affirmative. He then said to me, "You know, you ain't gonna ever graduate over there at A & M if you keep on driving back and forth to San Angelo." It just would not register that I could be a faculty member at Texas A & M. When I got home, it was clear that rural Texas was not going to be a place for me and my family.

I then took a position at California State University, Los Angeles (CSULA). It was our belief that we had escaped blatant racism when we arrived in liberal southern California. There were many experiences of negative racial incidents that I and my family encountered in the area, but the saving grace was that we were able to develop support systems in the greater Los Angeles black community. It was also a time when Randy Lindsey and I were reunited and what had begun as an important personal and professional relationship really sprouted. Seeing the "what" in terms of behaviors of whites and having a white male who serves as a cultural informant is helpful to be able to put many things in proper perspective. To have someone who was in touch with his social, emotional, psychological, and financial experiences as a privileged white male unpack that reality was unique.

Randy and I first worked together here in a private consulting firm that we established and that was dedicated to working to eradicate discrimination in all of its forms. One of the things that we determined was that the social consequences of discrimination could be very different from the personal consequences. Every individual who is discriminated against, for whatever reason, feels deeply aggrieved. However, the effects of systemic and institutional forms of oppression ranged all the way from forms of exclusion to genocide at its most negative end. One of the difficulties that people had in discussing these issues was that the conversation tended to lead to the "My pain is greater than your pain," and these proved to be fruitless debates, and too often, a lack of understanding the terms. While all negative attitudes, and more important behaviors, were directed toward others, there are different degrees to which the negative actions are taken.

We began our work with a few smaller school districts mostly in Los Angeles County. We focused on educational institutions because our professional training and experiences were in this arena. We also believed that people were not born with negative views about the various "isms," but rather they were learned phenomena. If they were learned, then the public school house could be the place where antiracist, antisexist, and other antis could also be taught. We also realized that in order for us to be successful in such a venture, the adults who populate public schools would have to have their belief and value systems challenged and find new ways to develop a view of cultural differences from a more reflective, deeper, and more positive position.

We encountered large numbers of educators who wanted to understand the diverse populations that they met at school each day, but most lacked knowledge and skills to make changes. We also soon discovered that there are deep-rooted structures embedded in all educational systems that make change difficult at best, and at some levels it seems impossible. Our work and the frustrations that we encountered served to pull us personally and professionally closer. We were able to share the pain that we experienced as we watched what was happening to children in classrooms, and what happened to us as we tried to challenge old theories, policies, practices, and procedures.

Our private consultant business slowly fell off and Randy was able to get a position as an assistant professor at CSULA. We drew on our prior experience in developing and delivering staff development in desegregating schools and applied for a training grant to train teachers and parents in Los Angeles Unified School District. We received $899,999 to be used over three years. We became aware that there was a similar effort taking place on a wider scale through the Region IX Desegregation Assistance Center. That Center was a federally funded project that was responsible for providing technical assistance and training for school districts in Arizona, California, Nevada, and Hawaii that were dealing with any problems incident to desegregation. We collaborated with the Center on some work in Los Angeles and provided some additional consulting for the Center to other districts in California.

We determined that the Center did not seem to have the commitment nor the skills that we had in addressing these issues, so in the next funding cycle we competed with the Far West Laboratory and were awarded the contract for the next three years, except we dropped Hawaii as a service area. Our experiences over this time period ranged all the way to having death threats made by some teachers in the central valley for proposing strategies to raise the achievement level of Latino students in their district. We were first told that the students were simply going to work as pickers in the fields so there was no need to worry about their educational attainment. When we pressed ahead, we were then told that if we were not careful, we would be "snuffed" before we could drive back to Los Angeles. Though the threats were not that overt, the level of resistance and the structural barriers that we encountered in the district were numerous and rigidly in place.

The central valley incident gave Randy and me cause to then discuss what it means to receive death threats as a person of color who is advocating for the basic rights of other people of color, and what it means to be a white male who receives the same death threat. Was it possible for either Randy or me to simply walk away from the situation? What did it mean when a group of white male teachers indicated that they would rather do violence to two people, one black and the other white, rather than even address making changes in attitudes and behaviors that would benefit Latino students? We were very clear that the threats were not idle. We had to take them seriously because there was a history of some Klan activity in the area and violent things had happened to people of color in the area. These were difficult discussions that challenged us to define not only what our commitment was to those students, but what our commitment was to each other. What would we do to protect or save one another in a life and death situation? How much trust did we really have? These are all nice theoretical conversations to have, but then we have to make a decision about how we are going to continue to serve the schools in that particular district. What did it mean to be called a "nigger lover" and have the ability to back out or even deny that you even knew any black people when your back is against the wall? What kind of commitment can a black male make to a white male who has made a commitment to push for social and educational change for students of color, knowing that the white male could, at any time, turn and walk away and fold his whiteness and privilege around him and be physically safe?

The story doesn't end here. The autobiography continues . . .

Appendix B

Randy's Cultural Autobiography

The following pages are a free-flowing, unplanned recollection of the development of my racial and cultural identity. I am crafting this introduction after having written the first draft of Early Family Life. At this early stage of chronicling the development of my cultural identity, the beginnings of my awareness of privilege and entitlement have emerged. As you'll note, Ray and I have each developed our own format for these autobiographies. We hope this will help demonstrate that there is no "one way" to do a cultural autobiography.

EARLY FAMILY LIFE

My first recollection of race was as a small child. I lived with my parents in a shotgun-style house that was located on the "other side" of the railroad tracks, behind a factory, in a neighborhood that was racially mixed. There were three groups we now call demographic groups—our labels were "colored people," the Irish, and we who were from "mid-southern" states. The period was the late 1940s and early 1950s. The black men and the southern white men worked in one of the three factories in town. My recollection is the Irish families were all related. They operated the trash collection business in town.

We all lived in this largely unimproved neighborhood. Yes, we had running water and some indoor plumbing, but the toilet was an outhouse in the back yard. In fact, one of the summer rituals was for the neighborhood men each summer to dig a new hole and to move the toilet. The bathtub was a Wheeling tub that my parents would fill with warm water heated on the stove for us to use. I never regarded it as a hard life because it wasn't. That was our life. Our house was clean and neat and I assume that was the case for all the other families in our neighborhood.

The odd thing was that we did very little visiting with those who were not like us. My father was always clear about the mistreatment of Negroes in the larger society. Neither of my parents went beyond eighth grade in their formal education. When he retired, my father had worked forty years in a foundry. My mom worked primarily in the home, except for a few years that she worked in a department store when my sister and I were in high school. During the time we lived in this neighborhood, my father freely walked up and down the street and, due to his gregariousness, walked in and out of everyone's homes. In contrast, my mother visited with no one and was not about to visit in the home of a black person. As you can imagine, black people were not invited to our home either. Directly across the street was the Smith family, a black family of two parents and several children. Ralph Jr. was my age and was in my class at Irving Elementary School. However, my mother would not permit him to play in our yard and I was never allowed to cross the street to his house. As a result, my thinking about matters of race developed when I was quite young.

Living in a home with parents who had different perspectives on race was disquieting and informing. My father was well known, and appeared to be liked, by Mr. and Mrs. Smith, as well as Mr. and Mrs. Franklin who lived down the street. Hmmm, I just thought of it, there was no apparent segregation—black and white families were interspersed together on our street. I guess the social pattern was where separation was maintained, at least in my family. While my father spoke against issues of racism, my mother was less generous.

Gender roles in our family were fairly traditional for the time. My father worked in the factory and my mother was a homemaker who worked in the home. Mom did the cooking, house cleaning, and lots of sewing and crocheting as hobbies. My dad's hobbies were the traditional male roles of hunting and fishing. In the evenings, we read or listened to the radio (I was in sixth grade when we got our first television). Though the work roles were traditional, my parents never deferred to one another due to gender roles. My sister, who is two years younger than I, fulfilled traditional female roles in high school for the 1950s—cheerleader, drum major, and homecoming queen. It was not until I was in high school that mom ventured out and took sales clerk jobs in local stores.

Religion and church played interesting roles in my formative years. Though I did not attend church until I was ten years old, religion was always present in conversation and the music that entered our homes and family get-togethers. My two most vivid images of religion are in seeming contrast: (1) gospel songs were present in our family get-togethers and in our radio music; and, (2) most often the Bible was "quoted" when a threat was deemed necessary (e.g., "that" is a sin; it says so in the Bible!).

It was in this earliest stage of my development that I became aware of differently abled people. There were men returning from World War II and the Korean War who had been wounded and disabled. Additionally, there was a man who was deemed by many to be of very low IQ but harmless. He could be seen at every high school football and basketball game and was known by all in town. He seemed to know everyone, too. He was just *there,* one of the many and varied people in town.

> **Summary of Personal Identity: Race, Gender and Social Class**
>
> • Awareness of being white—mother and father's differing value sets on race
> • First notion of Black anger
> • Gender roles were traditional for the era
>
> **Summary of Awareness of Race/Racism**
>
> • Dad's perspective on unfairness of disparate treatment of African Americans

VISITING WITH FAMILY IN EASTERN TENNESSEE

Both my mother and father's families had migrated to Illinois when they were children from mid-southern states. My father's family migrated in the late 1920s from an area close to Mammoth Cave, Kentucky. My mother's family had their roots in the Appalachian region of eastern Tennessee. Right after World War II the sun porch on the back of our house became the transitional home for many of mom's relatives who came to Kewanee in search of decent paying jobs. Some of the family stayed while others returned to Tennessee in ensuing years. This intercourse of family reconnected us with mom's aunts and uncles and facilitated most of our family vacations being with family in and around Kingsport, Tennessee. Our Tennessee family ranged from the very prosperous to some who were destitute. However, what I remember most are the hostile racial attitudes. Moreover, what I remember most vividly was my father's deft challenging of family members' attitudes. He was one of the few people who could do it and get away with it! The period was the mid to late 1950s. The modern civil rights movement was emerging. The *Brown* decision had rolled across the country like a veritable steamroller. In *my* community of marginalized, poor white people it raised all kinds of anger. I remember going to get my hair cut in Kewanee and having the barber say, "Well, if I have to cut 'their' hair, I have separate combs and brushes and I will burn them after they leave!"

Anyway, back to the Tennessee family. I remember my father being in a heated, but friendly debate (he was one of the few people in my life who could do both). Dad commented to a family member, "You are so prejudiced that you have labeled directions on the map to be east, west, south and *up south!*" Whatever heat he had stoked, he also caused to abate.

Gender roles in our extended family from Kentucky and Tennessee and the presence of religion were very similar to my experience in our hometown in Illinois. Men did men things and women did women things. Religion was comprised of things to fear, but gospel songs were uplifting. Formal religious training was largely absent. For that reason, my parents joined the First United Methodist Church. They thought it was time for my sister and me to be baptized and confirmed. I have wonderful recollections of the pastor at the time, Dr. Loyal M. Thompson, but the church experience was mostly social for me. I enjoyed the opportunity to be with other students my age and the history part of the Sunday school classes was usually interesting. I was aware that the kids in my school were of varying religions but it didn't seem to be an issue. However, adults could name the three Jewish families in town.

Summary of Personal Identity: Race, Gender, Social Class, and Religion

- Aware of polarizing effect of race in extended family relationships
- Aware of my father being *different* from other white people in acknowledging issues of race
- Aware that my father could communicate, seemingly effectively, with African Americans
- Aware of gender roles
- Aware that religious training was something "needed," much like going to school
- From my father I developed an appreciation for the lessons of studying history (e.g., he identified the Buffalo soldiers when I was a child; no teacher ever did such)

Summary of Awareness of Culture

- Initial awareness of modern civil rights movement
- Probably unacknowledged realization of the fact that white people had a choice whether or not to deal with issues of race

HIGH SCHOOL AND HARRY BABBITT

High school was essentially a blur for me. In fourth grade, my mom facilitated a move across town to get away from *them* and to a place where we had the toilet inside the house. I remember that being a good thing and have little recollection of missing the kids in the neighborhood. After all, I wasn't allowed to play with them, except at school as long as I remembered not to mention it at home. Oh yes, we did live in Tucson for most of my 8th grade year where I learned there were Mexicans, but I don't recall that being a divisive issue within my family. We did live next door to a family that included a boy about my age who had cerebral palsy. It was my first experience being near someone who needed full-time family care. My parents were quite friendly with his parents and my sister and I were taught not to fear his being different from us.

By high school, most of the black students had disappeared. There were two black students in my class and, though I knew them, there was virtually no contact.

My recollection of race was that it was invisible for me in high school. It was not part of my curriculum or my daily reality. My recollection of high school is somewhat idyllic—almost like *Happy Days*. I was not part of the in-group, but it was not a contentious experience either. I worked twenty to twenty-five hours (first as custodian's helper), then when I turned sixteen I became a stock boy (at the local A&P Food Store) and did well in school.

The high point for me was meeting Harry Babbitt. Dr. Babbitt was my freshman Spanish teacher. I ended up having him for three years of Spanish and one year of English. His contribution to my life was taking three other students and me on a driving tour of Mexico during Christmas, 1957. It was an experience that forever changed my life! I experienced a world that was different from anything I had ever experienced. We toured like middle class Mexicans, not Americans, visiting Mexico. We stayed in pleasant hotels where we practiced our Spanish. In Mexico City, I had my initial experience eating spaghetti with the accompaniment of a pasta spoon. We visited Chapultepec Palace and scaled the Pyramid of the Sun. We romped on the beach at Manzanillo—virtually alone on Christmas Day! We rode through the jungles on the way to Manzanillo and awoke one morning in my hammock to the cacophony of thousands of parrots. However, it was not all rosy as we also saw many examples of poverty that seemed more destitute than what we saw in the United States.

For me though, I saw another world. I saw a world of possibilities. I saw a world in which I wanted to be. Dr. Babbitt assumed that I was college material. I had no idea what that meant, but knew it was for me. I knew I was hungry for experiences that I could not see.

As a student, my awareness of gender roles was limited to the sports arena—boys were in interscholastic sports and girls participated in Girl's Athletic Association and as cheerleaders. Academically, girls and boys seemed to be well represented in science and mathematics and, more important, whom we recognized as the smartest kids. It seemed that boys and girls both went to college. Sexual orientation was a topic of sophomoric jokes.

Religion didn't appear to me to be an issue in my high school. However, it did occur in my home when my mother learned I was dating a Catholic girl. It was a muted objection that didn't last long, however I remember being stunned by the very raising of the issue. Over the years to ensue I was to learn that cross-cultural issues were often tested at the "dating age." The other occurrence was when my grandmother referred to her physician as "that Jewish doctor." It was never expressed in malevolence, only as a matter of fact as if it was part of his name. Christian physicians were not similarly identified.

When I walked across the stage for high school commencement, proverbially I had a one-way ticket out of Kewanee in my back pocket. At the time I thought I wanted to leave Kewanee behind. I now know that I wanted to leave bigotry behind.

Summary of Personal Cultural Identity

- Beginning awareness that the world was much larger than I suspected (i.e., much bigger than Kewanee or the limitations of my family's experience)

Summary of Awareness of Race/Racism

- Trip to Mexico opened up whole new world—exciting, yet knowledge that disparities extended well beyond US borders

WESTERN ILLINOIS UNIVERSITY

Due to a kidney ailment, I missed much of the second semester of my senior year in high school and had to delay entry into college a year while I healed. However, unlike many of my peers who delayed entry into college and never attended, I was very clear that I was *not* staying home!

In Kewanee and Macomb of the late 1950s and early 1960s, the Civil Rights Movement was something that didn't seem to touch me. It was on television and in the newspapers. I was aware of the lunch counter sit-ins and my dad and I talked about the bigotry and racism in our country, but it was not part of my daily life. Macomb, Illinois, didn't seem to be touched by the issues either. That was because I was ignorant of the presence of the issues in my midst.

At the beginning of my junior year at Western Illinois University (WIU), many of us who had chosen to avoid the Greek life were confronted with the need to develop well-rounded resumés. Our advisors strongly urged that we have something in our resumés to demonstrate to prospective employers that we were well rounded. So, I pledged a service fraternity associated with the Boy Scouts of America—the Mu Nu chapter of Alpha Phi Omega. As a service fraternity, we had two distinctive features—we were forbidden to have a house and we had black members. In my second semester I met John Elliott. John and I were social science education majors. Though I knew John—we had several classes together in our first two years—I never had a reason to really know him. After all, he was a gifted athlete, was exceptionally handsome, and seemed academically talented and out of my league. However, he pledged APO in the class after me (for the same resumé building reason) and the development of my racial identity was about to move to another level. Part of this development occurred during our time at WIU and part was to resume a few years later.

I am not sure where the new phase of my identity development began. John was the most artfully well-spoken person I had known to this point in my life. He had a rapier wit that could cut a person to the quick and, at the same time, a charming persona that made (white) people thank him for kicking their butts. Intuitively, I knew he was right. We did our student teaching the same quarter, Winter 1964, and upon returning to Macomb in March 1964 chose to room together off campus. "The education of Randy" was to continue at the new level. We both applied for campus jobs. We were both employed in food service. I served dessert in the women's dorm. John scrubbed pots and pans. I did not see the disparity until John pointed it out to me. Duhhhhh!

One evening we were going to play basketball. John was an accomplished athlete. I have been accused of many things in my life, yet being an athlete is not among them. For some reason, John saw fit to talk to me before the game. His caution was that in the heat of competition, I might utter the "dreaded racial slur" that he had never heard from me. I recall his being humored by my naiveté. His caution was that it would not be a problem if the word slipped out while we were playing one on one, but that I should exercise extreme caution and not let it slip in the presence of his black friends. Even now, I wonder why John invested that time and energy in me. However, I never made the miscue.

My last quarter at WIU was the summer of 1964. To fill my unit requirements, I took a master's level seminar in order to graduate. The seminar was Constitutional Law. During one session, the instructor who doubled as the department chair came in waving the local newspaper. He announced, "Ladies and gentlemen, yesterday the president signed a piece of legislation that will forever change your lives, The Civil Rights Act of 1964." He had no idea how prophetic he was to be about my life.

Summary of Personal Identity: Race and Social Class

- My whiteness became very personal—was able to see/know the privilege of being a white male in our society

Summary of Awareness of Race/Racism

- Competence takes a back seat to privilege

EARLY CAREER

John and I graduated August 1, 1964. I had a contract to teach in Kankakee and, to my recollection, John was still looking for a teaching position. I was surprised on my first day in Kankakee to learn that John also landed a position in Kankakee. The subtlety that was lost on me was that John had a much better resumé than I, but he got his position only when school was about to open.

I was single and John had married his college sweetheart, Joann, and they had begun their family with John Jr. It was when my principal was assisting me to look for housing, and he took me to a street map to orient me to the district, when I was to understand the racial bifurcation of the district. He outlined for me where I should look for housing and where I should avoid looking. John and Joann lived in the area I was to avoid. They had a lovely apartment; it was just that they had few choices.

In my teaching, I was not aware of formalized tracking until I saw the subtlety. My ninth grade ancient history sections were monolithically white, while my social studies classes were overrepresented with low-income white and black students. The former were college bound and the latter were high school bound. The blatant racism of some of the teachers was incredible. What was more incredible was the complicity of those of us who stayed silent.

Almost as oblivious was my awareness of the special education class in our junior high school building. I knew nothing of the students because they had their own classroom, their own teacher, and were identified by the use of terms such as EMR and TMR. There was little or no contact between the students from that classroom and our students. Too often, the students with special needs were the objects of jokes from both the regular education students and we educators.

In the summer 1966, I began my master's degree in Teaching of History at the University of Illinois where I took eight units in Negro American history. It was that eight units that formally changed my life forever. In one of the courses, I read all of the published works of James Baldwin and his novel, *Another Country,* has become the metaphor for my life. *Everything I learned was new!* I already had one degree in U.S. History, but nothing I learned at the U of I was a repeat—not even an allusion! It was all new. I was learning the history of a different United States. This was one of my first lessons in multiple perspectives!

It is important to remember that by this time Cheney, Schwermer, and Goodman had been killed by a white mob in Mississippi amid the drive to register black voters throughout the South, that the Watts riots had been the first of several urban riots, and that secondary schools were experiencing racially-based uprisings. As I brought my new knowledge to my high school classes, I was shocked at the resistance from some students. In retrospect, I was not aware at how racial attitudes were so deeply ingrained in our society. My naiveté continued unchecked. I guess the other half of the naiveté was the roiling awareness of the development of my own racial identity—privilege and entitlement.

> ## Summary of Personal Identity: Race and Social Class
>
> - Shocked to learn what I didn't know
> - Beginning to see the civil rights movement with faces
> - Students with special needs were part of an emerging awareness
>
> ## Summary of Awareness of Race/Racism
>
> - Though I was yet to learn the concepts—*omissions, distortions, and fallacious assumptions,* my study at U of I began the learning at deep levels
> - Racism as a concept began to develop in my mind
> - Urban unrest was real on television and for me had an historical context

HANFORD

My two years in Hanford contributed to my racial identify in one fundamental way. I had my first contact beyond the black-white racial dynamic. In Hanford, I had my first adult contact with two racial identity issues—Mexican Americans as immigrants and as historical residents, and Portuguese primarily as immigrants. With the former, it was as if they replaced African Americans as being an underclass in the way they were regarded in the schools and community. While there were many Americans of Mexican decent who were part of the mainstream social and economic dynamics of the community, most were part of the field labor pool. In contrast were the Portuguese who to the untrained eye appeared to be Latino, and they were much more likely to assimilate in two to three generations than were the Mexican Americans. Furthermore, the Portuguese were treated by the white community as more mainstream/assimilated.

This dynamic of who was assimilated in the school-tracking scheme became an education in privilege and entitlement. Unlike the subtlety practiced in Kankakee, the Hanford educators held tracking to a high value. The school had four tracks. From bottom to top they were—Z, Y, X and Advanced Placement. The lowest track, Z, was highly populated with Mexican Americans whereas they were almost invisible in the Advanced Placement sections. My first year at the school, as an unknown, I was assigned to two sections of Z, two sections of Y, and one of X. In the spring, I was informed that since I had proven myself in the first year, I would not have the Z track the next year. I was to learn that if one had a high proportion of their load assigned to the Z track, you most likely were not valued and that you were being pressured to leave.

In February 1970, I received a phone call from John Elliott that was to unfold the next chapter of my life. Kankakee was being pressured to desegregate their schools. John had been appointed as Community Services

Director for the district and the superintendent asked him to find a white person with whom he could work. In late spring, I interviewed and received the appointment to serve as Advisory Specialist to the Superintendent on matters related to school desegregation. John and I agreed we knew nothing about desegregation, but we would learn. Learn we did.

Summary of Personal Identity: Race and Social Class

- Beginning to recognize the disparities in schooling and how very few educators would confront inequities
- Beginning to understand *silence indicates consent*

Summary of Awareness of Race/Racism

- First awareness of the effects of school groupings (e.g., tracking)

BACK TO KANKAKEE AND INTO SCHOOL DESEGREGATION

The week my wife and I were leaving Hanford for our cross-country drive to Kankakee, I received a letter with no return address but with a Kankakee postmark. The message was comprised of cut out letters and the message warned me not to come to Kankakee. I would like to say that I was emboldened, but having seen how so many civil rights workers and others who supported integration efforts were treated, I was, in all candor, scared to death. I called John and told him of the letter and his response was *I told you it wouldn't be easy.* So I sucked it in, found a bit of resolve, and proceeded to Kankakee. I was never to hear about the letter again—in any form.

By the time I arrived, in mid-June 1970, John and the superintendent, Lee Grebner, had been working closely with representatives of the U.S. Office of Civil Rights to develop Kankakee's desegregation plan. John had cultivated deep, positive relationships with parents in the black and white communities to support the desegregation plan. The district had two high schools and two middle schools, so by moving the boundary lines the secondary schools could be desegregated relatively easily. There were eight elementary schools, one in the black community and seven in the white communities. The desegregation plan involved having the school in the black community and one in a white community turned into fourth and fifth grade centers and all other elementary schools were to be primary grade centers (i.e., Grades K–3). The result was that black kids were bused out of their communities in Grades K–3 and white students were bused into the two 4–5 grade centers, one of which was in the black community. In preparation for receiving children into Franklin School, centered in the black community, the district did an unprecedented face lifting to the school. (It is important to note that the black community supported the desegregation plan. The first year of the desegregation plan, 1970–71, vandalism at the school declined by 95 percent.) John and the mother's advisory group he formed implemented initial cross-town busing for desegregation without incident.

In the summer months of 1970 leading to the opening of school, I inherited the good planning that had been done by John and the superintendent. That summer we conducted two staff development activities. One series was led by Bea Young of the Illinois Commission on Human Relations (ICHR) and involved working with teachers to develop supplementary materials to the K–12 history and language arts materials that detailed the omissions, distortions, and fallacious assumptions in district text books. This activity provided me the opportunity to work with specialists provided by the ICHR and teachers from the district to develop supplementary materials for teacher use. My role during the year was to organize and deliver staff development sessions for teachers in appropriate use of the materials.

The second series of staff development sessions was with teacher leaders and administrators and was led by consultants from Ebony Management Associates. The sessions were comprised of a three week, five hour a day sensitivity session. The desired outcome was to develop us as a team in support of the desegregation effort.

These two staff development sessions were important to me personally and, I believe, to many other participants. However, I believe the sessions also served to galvanize resistance within school leadership and within the community. I was to learn that resistance to our work was latent in these early weeks and would surface later in the school year.

The fall of 1970 was surprisingly calm on the desegregation front. I spent much of my year working with school teams to learn how to use the companion materials. In retrospect, I am not certain they were widely used. However, there are anecdotal accounts that I recall vividly. One was an African American male elementary teacher who was so grateful for the materials. He confided in me that the information was mostly new to him. Another was a white female parent who was most disturbed by the materials. Her thinly veiled criticism was centered on the fact that "I" had capitalized "Black," but not white. She was resistant to the perspective that the former was a proper noun and the latter was not. She had gone through one of the volumes and had underlined all the passages with which she disagreed. The interesting thing was that she could provide no evidence; just that since it was new information to her it must have been fictionalized.

The peace ended in late spring, 1971, when riots broke out at the high schools. The riot at Eastridge High School was most devastating because a white male student was stabbed and several students were injured in melees. The principal called John and me in to assist, but had to eventually call in the police to clear the halls. John and I called ICHR who linked us with consultants from the Chicago YMCA who specialized in teen conflict. We took the suspension list and had the black students identify the white ringleaders and the white students to identify the black ringleaders. We took them off-site and worked thought the conflict. In two days of heavy, difficult confrontations the students began to realize they were not enemies. In fact, we uncovered the fact that the white students were goaded into action by a few of the white teachers.

If I have any clear recollection of my years in Kankakee it was the intractable racism of a few of the teachers. They were audacious enough to openly use racial slurs to describe black students and to publicly express doubt about the intellectual capability of black students. My companion recollection was that most of the rest of us conspired by our silence. It was this small group of teachers and administrators who were most surprised at my returning to Kankakee to work on the desegregation program. Though they knew of my friendship with John, they were surprised at my commitment to an antibiased curriculum and instruction program. I now had a forum from which to speak.

The upshot of the riots was that John and I prepared a report of our findings to deliver to the superintendent and board of education in June 1971. In the preceding April the community had elected a new member to the board. He was to prove himself to be deeply committed to undermining the desegregation efforts. The superintendent was aware that the small boardroom at the district office was not large enough for the large number of community members who would attend to hear our report, so the meeting was moved to the multipurpose room at Westridge High School. We sat on the front row facing members of the board. There were several hundred in attendance. In the minutes leading to the official beginning of the meeting, there was a hum among those in attendance. All of a sudden the room went quiet. About fifty state police in riot gear entered the room and assumed positions on the periphery of the room. I was to find out later that the superintendent was not involved in the decision and was as surprised as anyone else in the room. We were to learn later that the new board member, who was an executive in an international corporation that had a plant in Kankakee, had worked with an elementary principal to make the decision to involve the state troopers in our meeting. In a subsequent meeting, this board member, in collusion with other members, created the position of Executive Superintendent and successfully appointed the elementary principal into the position. The superintendent was shocked, as were the rest of us.

The next day, the new Executive Superintendent told me that he had to rely on John and me to continue our program. He told me that I had legitimacy in the black community that he wanted to support. Concurrent with these events I was developing an application for continued funding of our efforts. At the direction of my program officer, I created a needs assessment in which I documented disparities in the treatment of black and white students—retention in first and eighth grades, suspension and expulsion rates. At the end of the summer, the superintendent told me he would not submit the application, effectively ending my employment because my data made the district look bad!

During that year, November 1970 to be precise, I had attended the initial training of advisory specialists conducted by Jim Barnes and staff from the University of Hartford. It was at this training that I met Ray Terrell. Meeting Ray was to change my life forever in very constructive ways; we developed a very special friendship. During that school year he came to Kankakee to consult for me and I conducted a session for him at the Princeton City School District in suburban Cincinnati. During the spring, 1971, Ray had offered me a position with him, which I turned down as I was committed to Kankakee. I was relieved to find out in August the position was unfilled and by early September 1971, I was living in Cincinnati and was a member of Ray's desegregation team.

Summary of Personal Identity: Race and Social Class

- Any naiveté that I had disappeared in Kankakee
- Intense pressures not to do anything effective
- White supporters of this work were few and far between and were overwhelmed by the hostility and the indifference of other whites
- Many African Americans were initially suspicious of me, but increased in confidence when John vouched for me and my values

Summary of Awareness of Race/Racism

- The deep, seemingly intractability of racism and the unwillingness of most people to admit racial disparities were anything more than personal ambition

PRINCETON CITY SCHOOL DISTRICT

Ray wanted me to work with two primarily white communities—Heritage Hill and Springdale. I served as a community school director supervising programs that were consistent with community development efforts conceptualized by the Mott Foundation in Flint, Michigan. In reality, the position provided me transparent *cover* to work with Ray on the desegregation team. I loved the work, the camaraderie, and working with Ray. It was in this year that I began my journey to understanding racism and developing my identity as a white male in this society.

Ray involved team members in readings, discussions, and conferences in which we plumbed our thoughts, feelings, and notions about race and class. I was able to draw on my academic work about Negro American History, the curricular materials we developed in Kankakee, and my deep resentment over what had happened in Kankakee. It was at this stage in my development that I made a powerful association. Even today I can't locate its genesis, whether Ray pushed me to the realization or if it was the confluence of so much stuff. My realization about what had happened in Kankakee was that I had the choice of walking away, licking my wounds, maintaining an air of self-righteousness, and living a comfortable middle class lifestyle. Or, I could stay engaged with the issues and do what I could to make life better for myself and others. I chose the latter.

I became fascinated with trying to understand *white, institutional racism*. I could identify racism. I could give examples of racism. I could not *understand* it. I read the Kerner Report. I studied Pat Bidol's curriculum *Developing New Perspectives on Race*. I pored over Abraham Citron's monograph *The Rightness of Whiteness: The Malformation of the Mind of the White Child in the Suburban Ghetto*. Robert Terry's *For Whites Only* became my companion. I was beginning to understand that knowing *whiteness* helped me understand why all of the information in my Negro American history courses was new. My insights transcended the personal knowledge of white culpability to a beginning awareness of the systemic nature of racism. Samuel Yette's *The Choice* helped me to see that white people *always* had the choice to deal with issues of racism, whereas for black people dealing with racism was/is a natural course of events.

During our year together in Princeton, I learned more about my white racial identity. For one thing, I became comfortable for the first time with my social class. For some reason, I had developed the desire to conceal this fact from others and myself. I vividly recall two sixth grade lessons: In the first, our teacher, for a lesson on nutrition, had us write down what we ate for our three meals. I was reluctant to include gravy in my description for fear that *gravy* was not eaten by others and would betray my lower class status. In the second experience, my teacher had graded me a straight "A" in all subjects for the first four grading periods. During the fifth grading period he visited our modest home after which he graded me a straight "B" in all subjects. His explanation to my father was that we were going into junior high school the next year and he wanted us to know it would be more difficult. At the end of the year, he added a course titled "Writing" to our grade report cards and entered a grade of "B" retroactively to all grading periods, effectively interrupting the straight "A" designation of the first four grading periods. It was interesting to learn that this only occurred for those of us from modest backgrounds. My peers from "nicer" homes continued with uninterrupted straight "A" grades. I was not unclear on my social class.

Now that I am thinking about it, as a sophomore at WIU, in my introductory sociology class, Dr. Jane Stull had us find our social class on a nine-level schema. Each of the three social classes was further subdivided into three groups. After searching for my parents' level of education and employment I was stunned to learn that I was in middle-lower class. I can still recall the mild shock and looking around at my classmates in embarrassment, hoping they didn't see my results. Though I had the distasteful experiences in my sixth grade class, it was this experience that made it a reality—I was lower class.

Irrespective of "getting in touch with my own social class," I was learning in Princeton with Ray, Nancy, Eric, Tom, and Don about the reality that when we confront racism, all boats rise. One of the things that continues to perplex me today is how I was able to make that connection—either emotionally or intellectually! So many of my colleagues, it appeared to me, examined the same issues only to become defensive about disparity and chose to use that against black Americans. I assume it was my relationship with Ray and John that kept me from falling into that trap?

The most vivid recollection from my year in Princeton with Ray came at the end of the year. In August 1972, Ray had accepted a position with Texas A & M and I was moving into the district office to assume his staff development responsibilities. The school district had elected a new member to the school board. She had run for the school board representing the White Citizens of Sharonville on an anti-busing platform. To make their organization palpable, they changed the name to Princeton Parent Action Council. They greatly disliked the superintendent, Robert E. Lucas, because they thought he sold the district on the desegregation plan which included the development of a middle school in Sharonville that involved busing in of black children from Woodlawn.

At the request of Dr. Lucas and the new board member, I attended an evening meeting of the PPAC to provide a progress report on the desegregation plan. I was welcomed as an alternative to Dr. Lucas since he could not be trusted. I have two specific recollections of the evening. After my comments and update, I invited questions. In response to one of the questions, I commented that members of the organization were thought by many to be allies of the Ku Klux Klan. A man who sat impassively in the third row and wore mercury lens aviator-style sunglasses through the meeting (much like the guard in the movie, *In the Heat of the Night),* commented, "It is more than 'thought to be!'" I can still feel the chill that ran through my body at his comment.

After they were through with me, my host came to the microphone and said that there would be a short refreshment intermission. It was during this time, the host announced, that I would leave and afterwards their business meeting would continue as a closed business meeting. The only door was at the other end of the room and I had to make my way through the crowd with no one making way for me. I had to weave around and through the group. What I recall is that these were *my people.* In another setting, they could have been relatives—close relatives. And they—like me, working class white people, communicated such antipathy for me. Of course, they didn't know me or my roots in nearby Kentucky. I was another white liberal trying to extend this social experiment with their children. It was a long walk to the door. It felt like a gauntlet, though no one commented or touched me. However, I was fully aware of how other similar activities had fared in both the north and south. Scared to death— you bet!

I proceeded to the district office where Lucas and Ray were waiting for me. They appeared to be relieved, as was I. However, as I recount my own feelings of the evening, I never doubted how this was adding to my racial identity. In some way, I saw the people in that hall that evening as much victims of the social/racial dynamics as were black Americans.

What I was able to recognize is that they could not see their complicity in their own underclassness. By making black people their enemies, they were accepting their own position within the society. *They may have been poor, but, by god, they weren't black!*

In my second year at Princeton, Ray had left to take a faculty position at Texas A & M. Nancy, Don, Eric, and Tom had been assigned to schools throughout the district. Superintendent Lucas elevated me to take a portion of Ray's work—staff development. It was an undistinguishable year. I continued my learning about racism, attending conferences, getting a divorce, and searching for meaning in my life. In retrospect, I can see where I was struggling with my own racial and social class identity, but it was to take several more years before it made sense to me.

During that year I had my initial sexual orientation experience. All of the teachers new to the district were required to take my several session course, "Developing New Perspective on Race." The course started well and all who were supposed to be in attendance did so each week until about the sixth week when one of the members quit coming. After a few missed sessions, I called him to inquire about his absences. He asked for a private meeting to discuss his concerns with the course. We met at a local bar where he proceeded to tell me how much he enjoyed the course but his big fear was that our climate of openness might make him feel too comfortable and he might share with the group that he was gay. I was dumbfounded. Though I was well aware of issues of sexual orientation, I had never (knowingly) talked with a gay person. I was immediately aware of my feelings of uneasiness in his presence. The meeting ended amicably and he agreed to return to the course but would probably be reticent to be open. He conceded that if he revealed his sexual orientation that he would most likely be released from his contract. He was most likely correct.

I recall at the time being conflicted. Part of me was deeply bothered that people experienced the types of overt discrimination that my gay colleague described to me. I didn't want him to lose his job as I regarded him to be an excellent teacher. At the same time, I was fully aware of my feelings of avoidance. Later, I had occasion to raise my colleague's dilemma with Ray and Nancy and during the discussion I shared my feelings of avoidance. Ray and Nancy pushed me very hard and asked me, "What gives you the right to decide which equity issues you agree to support and which ones you don't? Isn't that an ultimate form of entitlement?" That heated discussion rings in my ears thirty years later. I was beginning to see the benefit of having cultural informants as a means to be able to see my own assumptions.

In late August 1973, I accepted a phone call from James Frasher at Georgia State University (GSU) that took me to the next stage of my personal development. As fortuitous as many stages of my life had been, I fell into an opportunity. Earlier in the year, I had made a presentation at the desegregation center at Kent State University. Georgia State had received an Education Professions Development Act (EPDA) grant to train

PhD candidates as change agents. In the trading of votes that members of the U. S. Senate had to do to support funding the EPDA, three positions had to go to residents of Ohio. The dean at GSU had a brother who was dean at Kent. It was the last minute and they needed nominations of people who could make the move in less than three weeks. The dean at Kent had, unknown to me, been in my audience. By mid-September I was a resident of Atlanta and enrolled in the PhD program at GSU.

Summary of Personal Identity: Race and Social Class

- Crystallization of my social class identity
- Understanding of what I could do, within the white communities, to address racism
- Learning of my own homophobia and the existence of heterosexism
- Developing value for cultural informancy—my learning from others
- Initial awareness of privilege and entitlement—how I could be a cultural informant! It was so much a part of me, I couldn't see it!

Summary of Awareness of Systemic Oppression

- Deeper awareness of how dominant society uses race against low-income white people to value skin color over financial status
- Burgeoning awareness of heterosexism

GEORGIA STATE UNIVERSITY

To say the move to Georgia was fortuitous is a great understatement. After six years as a teacher and three highly eventful years as an administrator working with school desegregation, to have the opportunity to step out of reality and to reflect, learn, and assess was a luxury! I was one of the doctoral candidates who entered the program with a clear focus. I wanted to learn as much as possible about racism—its properties, how people were penalized, and how people benefited.

What I didn't know until getting to Atlanta was that Alonzo Crim had become superintendent, the first black superintendent of a major school district in the United States. I was fortunate to have my fieldwork placement with one of his five area superintendents, Alvin Dawson, who was also in the PhD program. Dr. Crim and Mr. Dawson provided me much support to continue my professional development work with their teachers and administrators.

The significant contribution to my racial identity was found in the work of Joel Kovel, *A Psychohistory of White Racism*. Kovel provided the conceptual framework for my dissertation and the basis for my personal evolution of identity. Kovel provided me with the words to understand racism at a systemic level. As a student of history, I could relate to Kovel's description of racism—*the activity in history and culture in which races may be created, oppressed, and fantasied without the aid of bigots.* That was it! The white folks of the Princeton Parent Action Council were, no doubt, bigots. Probably many were involved in acts too terrible to mention, but racism would persist without their presence.

Summary of Personal Identity: Race and Social Class

- A meta-cognitive period of my life
- I became reflective about who I was as a cultural being
- Ray was immensely helpful in seeing my social class as a positive part of me

Summary of Awareness of Race/Racism

- Race and racism had definitions! They had properties to be described and explained and used in working in PreK–12 schools

---

LOS ANGELES

In 1974, Ray had moved from Texas to Cal State, Los Angeles. After graduating from GSU, I moved to L. A. to work with Ray. We began a consulting agency, the Center for Cultural Training (CCT), which morphed three years later into Terrell, Lindsey, Trives and Associates (TLT). I also began that fall teaching adjunct at Cal State, Los Angeles. Over the next few years, my work on antiracism continued to evolve. My early success with CCT and TLT was due to contracts with agencies in support of Los Angeles and Inglewood's desegregation plans. My success as an adjunct at Cal State was attributed to the fact that I could "successfully" teach the diversity course that Ray had designed, Social and Political Forces Affecting Education. In time I was able to convince the department chair that I could teach the leadership and decision-making courses, too. He was an ally and was embarrassed that I had been pigeon holed into only one type of course. However, I was becoming aware of the uniqueness of having a white guy teach the course in a manner that communicated to and with students from every demographic group.

In our days at CCT, TLT, and Cal State Ray and I evolved a distinctive training style. In preparing to work with schools, we scripted who would say what. As an example, we decided it was a stronger voice for me to define and describe institutional racism. Our thinking was that session participants often viewed African Americans describing racism from a vested interest perspective, so when I took that role it was more difficult for participants to challenge my having a vested interest. Also, it was important to us that racism be viewed as a *white problem* that needed to be deconstructed by white people. Within the white problem paradigm, in working with groups we took great care to emphasize that the needed deconstruction involved all educators, irrespective of their cultural groups, because we are all players in the same system (that was constructed by white America).

Likewise, when describing the language and life styles of African American children and youth, Ray was viewed as being the stronger, better informed voice. While we, among the two of us, believed that we could be interchangeable on most topics, we planned our comments around what we viewed to be the needs of session participants.

When Ronald Reagan became president of the United States, I knew our days of having a successful firm that relied on federal grants had come to an end. I assumed a one-year faculty position in 1980, which later evolved into a tenure track appointment. When Ray became Dean of the School of Education, I took over the project director position with the three-state regional desegregation center, the Regional Assistance Center for Educational Equity (RACEE). For five years, I worked with colleagues to provide services to school districts in California, Arizona, and New Mexico. It was during this time period that I began to learn the commonalities among systems of oppression—sexism, ableism, and heterosexism. One of my new colleagues, Kikanza Nuri Robins, and Ray continued to push me to deal with my sexism and homophobia. It was a painful process and I wanted to stay tied to what I knew most and best—race and issues of racism. Kikanza and Ray would have none of it. They challenged me by asking what made me think that as an adherent to equity that I had the right to pick and choose my "isms." That was a helpful and powerful learning that continues to unfold!

By this time, I had infused issues of equity into my courses and consulting, irrespective of the context. I was convinced that the systemic nature of oppression was they had to be dealt with both in context and separately. For our curriculum, that meant the diversity course *and* the infusion of equity throughout the curriculum. It was not an easy transition for my colleagues. There was resistance in the recasting of courses and in searches for faculty members.

Project Regional Assistance Center for Educational Equity (RACEE) provided resources and the vehicle to extend the work. It also provided the space for us to begin to conceptualize what was to become, ten years later, our work in cultural proficiency. I developed a regional profile known to school districts and the California Commission on Teacher Credentialing (CCTC). It appeared that I could get different forums to continue the work of equity. I experienced most of the work of school districts and agencies such as CCTC, California Teachers Association (CTA), Association of California School Administrators (ACSA), etc. as lip service. It drove me nuts but I kept focused on the fact that I had a choice—I could deal with the issues or I could walk away. Knowing that I could walk away was always the sobering part of systemic oppression for me. My colleagues who directly felt racism, sexism, or heterosexism could not walk away from it, for it was ever present in their lives. My *Appalachian male* identity was, for all intents and purposes, invisible.

Summary of Personal Identity: Race and Social Class

- Began to recognize how and where I could make a difference (e.g., hiring at Cal State; overhauling our Educational Administration (EDAD) curriculum; work with PreK–12 schools)
- Began to appreciate my role in higher education to shape policy and practice

Summary of Awareness of Race/Racism

- Began to see common denominators among systems of oppression

CULTURAL PROFICIENCY—PUTTING IT ALL TOGETHER

It must have been about 1990 that Kikanza attended a session in Washington, DC, where she learned of Terry Cross's *Cultural Competence* work. In Kikanza's words, *I knew I was opposed to systems of oppression; Cultural Competence gave me a framework in what I was "for."*

Cross's construct of cultural competence includes two bullets of information that he identified to be barriers—unawareness of the need to adapt, and a sense of entitlement. Those two phrases are the sum total of Cross's description of the barriers to cultural competence. More important, these two phrases became the springboard for my initial thinking/writing with Ray and Kikanza. The Five Essential Elements of Cultural Competence provided the framework for what can/should be. Cross had cast the elements as standards for policy/practice and value/behavior formulation. The barriers were the obstructions with which I was most informed and had the greatest passion.

It is in this latter part of my career that I began to see the connections with issues of ableness, faith, and social class in the same manner that I had developed an awareness of the oppression experienced by people due to their race, ethnicity, gender, sexual orientation, and social class. Cross's identifying the unawareness of the need to adapt as one of the barriers to being effective in cross-cultural interactions continues to inform my growth and learning.

Yet, I struggled in the early writing. I had not learned to write well. Kikanza and Delores were patient, supportive, and helpful. My struggle wasn't just with the mechanics of writing. I am learning that so much of my existence had moved into being *cerebral*. One of the ways I have learned to cope with my personal issues of underclassness and revulsion over issues of racism, was to *know* so much that I overwhelmed opposing views with the sheer anti-intellectual nature of bias and discrimination. In the last fifteen years, I have learned to put a face on the issues—often my own issues of feeling that I don't fit in. I have consciously used this insight about myself to continue the work. It seems (to me) to be effective.

Cross's work has helped me to crystallize many learnings, in no apparent order:

- It is necessary to work on values/behaviors and policies/practices simultaneously.
- The continuum provides a perspective for dealing with values/behaviors and policies/practices.
- The *inside-out* approach, for individuals and organizations, is profound work.
- Systems most often don't do the good work unless goaded or otherwise forced to do so. Evidence is the current school reform efforts that utilize disaggregated data. The data have been available all this time. Why were/are schools resistant to the voices within that were pointing out disparities and unfairness.
- Facility with cultural proficiency works only in the context of doing the work of the organization; it can't become an end in itself.
- Confronting systems of oppression is a life-long process of personal self-examination and moving organizations.
- I have developed a historical context for this work.
- I made choices for equity, not the other paths that were present.
- The presence of significant people as cultural informants in my life has been *the* catalyst for my personal growth.

References and Further Readings

Acuna, Rodolfo. (1987). *Occupied America* (3rd ed.). Boston: Pearson.

Anderson, Peggy. (2007). Nelson Mandela. *Great quotes from great leaders.* Naperville, IL: Simple Truths, 69.

Armstrong, Karen. (1993). *A history of God: The 4000-year quest of Judaism, Christianity and Islam.* New York: Random House.

Association for Supervision and Curriculum Development. (2007). Title IX turns 35. *Education Update, 49* (12).

Baca, Leonard, & Almanza, Estella. (1991). *Language minority students with disabilities.* Reston, VA: Council for Exceptional Children.

Banks, James. (1999). *An introduction to multicultural education* (3rd ed.). Needham, MA: Allyn & Bacon.

Bennett, Christine. (2001). Genres of research in multicultural education. *Review of Educational Research, 71* (2), 171–217.

Berliner, David. (2005). Our impoverished view of educational reform. *Teachers College Record.* August 02, 2005. Retrieved August 26, 2005, from http://www.tcrecord.org

Bochenek, Michael, & Brown, A. Widney. (2001). *Hatred in the hallways: Violence and discrimination against lesbian, gay, bisexual and transgender students in U.S. schools.* New York: Human Rights Watch.

Brown, Dee. (1971). *Bury my heart at wounded knee.* New York: Holt Rinehart and Winston.

Bush vows New Orleans will rise again. (2005, September 16). *North County Times.* A7.

CampbellJones, Brenda (2002). *Against the stream: White men who act in ways to eradicate racism and white privilege/entitlement in the United States of America.* Unpublished doctoral dissertation, Claremont Graduate University.

Carter, Thomas P. (1970). *Mexican Americans in school: A history of educational neglect.* New York: College Entrance Examination Board.

Clark, Kenneth B. & Clark, Mamie K. (1950). Emotional factors in racial identification and preference in Negro children. *Journal of Negro Education, 19,* 341–350.

Coleman, James S. (1966). *Equality of educational opportunity study.* Washington, DC: U.S. Department of Health, Education, and Welfare, Office of Education/National Center for Education Statistics.

Collins, Jim. (2001). *Good to great.* New York: Collins.

Cross, Terry, Bazron, Barbara, Dennis, Karl, & Isaacs, Mareasa. (1989). *Toward a culturally competent system of care* (Vol. 1). Washington, DC: Georgetown University Child Development Program, Child and Adolescent Service System Program.

Cummins, Jim. (1988). From multicultural to anti-racist education: An analysis of programmes and practices in Ontario. In Tove Skuttnabb-Kangas and Jim Cummins (Eds.), *Minority education.* Philadelphia: Multilingual Matters.

Deloria, Vine. (1969). *Custer died for your sins: An Indian manifesto.* New York: Macmillan.

Delpit, Lisa. (1996). *Other people's children: Cultural conflict in the classroom.* New York: New Press.

Dewey, John. Wisdom Quotes. Retrieved October 9, 2006, from http://www.wisdomquotes.com/001897.html

Edmonds, Ron. (1979). Some schools work and more can. *Social Policy, 9* (5), 3.

Education Trust. (2006). *Education watch the nation: Key education facts and figures, achievement, attainment and opportunity from elementary school through college.* Washington, DC: Education Trust, Inc. Retrieved November 24, 2007, from http://www2.edtrust.org/edtrust/summaries2006/states.html

Franklin, John Hope, & Moss, Alfred A. Jr. (1988). *From slavery to freedom: A history of Negro Americans* (6th ed.). New York: McGraw Hill.

Freire, Paolo. (1987). *Pedagogy of the oppressed.* New York: Continuum.

Fullan, Michael. (2003). *The moral imperative of school leadership.* Thousand Oaks, CA: Corwin Press.

Galarza, Ernesto. (1971). *Barrio boy: The story of a boy's acculturation.* Notre Dame, IN.: The University of Notre Dame Press.

Gardner, John W. (1961). *Excellence: Can we be equal and excellent too?* New York: Harper Row.

Gilligan, Carol. (1983). *In a different voice.* Cambridge, MA: Harvard University Press.

Gollnick, Donna M., & Chinn, Philip C. (2006). *Multicultural education in a pluralistic society.* Philadelphia: Wharton School Publishing, Pearson.

Handlin, Oscar. (1954). *The American people in the twentieth century.* Cambridge, MA: Harvard University Press.

Hilliard, Asa. (1991). Do we have the will to educate all children? *Educational Leadership, 40* (1), 31–36.

Human rights code. (Province of Ontario, Canada). Retrieved December 10, 2007, from http://www.elaws.gov.on.ca/html/statutes/english/elaws_statutes_90h19_e.htm

Hudson, J. Blaine. (1999). Affirmative action and American racism in historical perspective. *The Journal of Negro History, 84* (3), 260–274.

Jencks, Christopher, Smith, Marshall, Acland, Henry, & Bane, Mary Jo. (1972). *Inequality: A reassessment of family and schooling in America.* New York: Basic Books.

Kousser, J. Morgan. (1984). Suffrage. In Greene, J. P. (Ed.), *Encyclopedia of American political history: Studies of the principal movements and ideas.* (Vol. 1–3) (pp. 1236–1258). New York: Scribner.

Kozol, Jonathan. (1991). *Savage inequalities.* New York: Crown Publishers.

Kozol, Jonathan. (2005). *The shame of a nation.* New York: Crown Publishers.

Kozol, Jonathan. (2007). *Letters to a young teacher.* New York: Crown Publishers.

Krashen, Stephen D. (1987). *Principles and practice in second language acquisition.* New York: Prentice-Hall International.

Ladson-Billings, Gloria. (2005). *Beyond the big house: African American educators on teacher education.* New York: Teachers College Press.

Landsberg, Mitchell & Blume, Howard. (2007). Schools chief seeks end to learning gap: Jack O'Connell earns praise for his candor on sensitive subject: Persistent lagging achievement among blacks and Latinos. *Los Angeles Times,* August 19, 2007. Retrieved September 16, 2007, from http://pqasb.pqarchiver.com/latimes/access/1322022581.html

Latham, Peter S., Latham, Patricia H., & Mandlawitz, Myrna R. (2008). *Special education law.* Boston: Pearson.

Lindsey, Delores B., Martinez, Richard S., & Lindsey, Randall B. (2007). *Culturally proficient coaching: Supporting educators to create equitable schools.* Thousand Oaks, CA: Corwin Press.

Lindsey, Randall B., Roberts, Laraine, M. & CampbellJones, Franklin. (2005). *The culturally proficient school: An implementation guide for school leaders.* Thousand Oaks, CA: Corwin Press.

Lindsey, Randall B., Nuri Robins, Kikanza, & Terrell, Raymond D. (2003). *Cultural proficiency: A manual for school leaders* (2nd ed.). Thousand Oaks, CA: Corwin Press.

Lindsey, Randall B., Graham, Stephanie M., Westphal Jr., R. Chris, & Jew, Cynthia L. (2008). *Culturally proficient inquiry: A lens for identifying and examining educational gaps.* Thousand Oaks, CA: Corwin Press.

Loewen, James W., (1995). *Lies my teacher told me: Everything your American history textbook got wrong.* New York: New Press.

Manglitz, Elaine, Johnson-Bailey, Juanita, & Cervero, Ronald M. (2005). Struggles of hope: How white adult educators challenge racism. *Teachers College Record, 107* (6), 1245–1274. Retrieved October 26, 2007 from http://www.tcrecord.org

Marzano, Robert J., Pickering, Debra J., & Pollock, Jane E. (2001). *Classroom instruction that works: Research-based strategies for increasing student achievement.* Alexandria, VA: Association for Supervision and Curriculum Development.

McWilliams, Carey. (1968). *North from Mexico: The Spanish speaking people of the United States.* Westport, CT: Greenwood Press.

Miller, Neil. (2006). *Out of the past: Gay and lesbian history from 1869 to the present.* New York: Alyson Books.

Milner IV, H. Richard. (2007). Race, culture, and research positionality: Working through dangers seen, unseen, and unforeseen. *Educational Researcher, 36* (7), 388–400.

National Center for Educational Statistics. (2005). *Digest of education statistics, 2005.* Washington, D. C.: Institute of Education Sciences.

NCLB, No Child Left Behind Act. (2001). Retrieved September 5, 2007, from http://www.ed.gov/nclb

Nichols, Sharon L. & Berliner, David C. (2007). *Collateral damage: How high stakes testing corrupts America's schools.* Cambridge, MA: Harvard University Press.

Obama urges moving past 'old racial wounds.' (2008, March 19) *The Los Angeles Times.* A10.

Palmer, Parker. (1997). *The company of strangers, Christians and the renewal of America's public life.* New York: The Crossroad Publishing Company.

Perie, Marianne, Moran, Rebecca, & Lutkus, Anthony D. (2005). *NAEP 2004 trends in academic progress: Three decades of student performance in reading and mathematics (NCES 2005–464).* U.S. Department of Education, Institute of Education Sciences, National Center for Education Statistics. Washington, DC: Government Printing Office.

Reeves, Douglas. (2006). *The learning leader: How to focus school improvement for better results.* Alexandria, VA: Association for Supervision and Curriculum Development.

Reiter, L. (1989). Sexual orientation, sexual identity, and the question of choice. *Clinical Social Work Journal, 17,* 138–150.

Richardson, John G. (1980). Variation in date of enactment of compulsory school attendance laws: An empirical inquiry. *Sociology of Education, 53* (3), 153–163.

Rivers, Dana. (2007). Personal communication, October 6, 2007.

Sadker, Myra, & Sadker, David. (1994). *Failing at fairness: How America's schools cheat girls.* New York: Charles Scribner's Sons.

Schein, Edgar. (1989). *Organizational culture and leadership: A dynamic view.* San Francisco: Jossey-Bass.

Schimmel, David, Fischer, Louis, & Stellman, Leslie R. (2008). *School law: What every educator should know.* New York: Pearson.

Schon, Donald A. (1983). *The reflective practitioner.* New York: Basic Books.

Seguine, Denise. (2006). Personal communication, October 3, 2006.

Senge, Peter, Cambron, Nelda H., McCabe, Timothy Lucas, Kleiner, Art, Dutton, Janis, & Smith, Bryan. (2000). *Schools that learn: A fifth discipline fieldbook for educators, parents, and everyone who cares about education.* New York: Doubleday.

Shapiro, Joan Poliner, & Stefkovich, Jacqueline A. (2005). *Ethical leadership and decision making* (2nd ed.). Mahwah, NJ: Lawrence Erlbaum Associates.

Singleton, Glen E., & Linton, Curtis. (2006). *Courageous conversations about race: A field guide for achieving equity in schools.* Thousand Oaks, CA: Corwin Press.

Sleeter, Christine E., & Grant, Carl A. (2007). *Making choices for multicultural education: Five approaches to race, class, and gender* (2nd ed.). New York: Macmillan.

Takaki, Ron. (1989). *Strangers from a different shore: A history of Asian Americans,* Boston: Little Brown & Co.

Takaki, Ron. (1993). *A different mirror: A history of multicultural America,* Boston: Little Brown & Co.

Townley, Arthur J., & Schmeider-Ramirez, June H. (2007). *School law: A California perspective* (3rd ed.). Dubuque, IA: Kendall-Hunt.

Trumbull, Elise, Rothstein-Fisch, Carrie, Greenfield, Patricia M., & Quiroz, Blanca. (2001). *Bridging cultures between home and school: A guide for teachers.* Mahwah, NJ: Lawrence Erlbaum Associates.

Trumbull, Elise. (2005). Language and assessment. In Elise Trumbull & Beverly Farr, *Language and learning: What teachers need to know.* Norwood, MA: Christopher-Gordon.

Unger, Harlow G. (2001). Compulsory education. *Encyclopedia of American Education* (2nd ed.), 275–276.

Wheatley, Margaret J. (1994). *Leadership and the new science.* San Francisco: Berrett-Koehler.

Wheatley, Margaret J. (2002). *Turning to one another: Simple conversations to restore hope to the future.* San Francisco: Berrett-Koehler.

Zinn, Howard. (2003). *A people's history of the United States: 1492 to present.* New York: Harper Collins.

Index

CORWIN PRESS

The Corwin Press logo—a raven striding across an open book—represents the union of courage and learning. Corwin Press is committed to improving education for all learners by publishing books and other professional development resources for those serving the field of PreK–12 education. By providing practical, hands-on materials, Corwin Press continues to carry out the promise of its motto: **"Helping Educators Do Their Work Better."**